WHO
DO YOU
TRUST?

WHO
DO YOU
TRUST?

A Compilation of Sermons by
PATRICK D. MCGOLDRICK

Edited by Tim Stevens
Foreword by Bob Johnson II

Cover design by Volacious Media
Interior design by Katherine@theDESKonline.com

Printed in the United States of America

Contents

Acknowledgments

On October 16, 2012, I put the word out on LeadingSmart.com:

I am launching a book project to help Patrick's legacy continue. He has selected a compilation of sermons that he has preached in recent years—including his final sermon from this past April—and we are going to publish these in a book. These are sermons that define what he believes and will help his message live on—now that he can't speak, and later when he is no longer on this earth.

I was floored by the response. From all across the country, people asked if they could help. Some were good friends of Patrick's; others had never met him but became captivated by his story. Scores volunteered, so many that I couldn't utilize everyone. But I do want to take the time to thank those who made the book possible.

A huge thanks to Shelly Alley, Valerie Angello, David Arnold, Krista Back, Stephanie Bens, Jason Coplen, Amber Cox, Stephanie Dilley, Mike Farrell, Linda Herhuth, Ann Lightbody, Jennifer Peck, Brittany Riblet, and Karen Stevens. And a special shout-out to Amanda Harris and Liz Kaynor, who helped on several chapters while deadlines were looming.

I'm also grateful to Ben Stroup (benstroup.com), who gathered the strength of his entire creative group to edit, design, and lay out the book. His involvement assured the professional completion to this grass roots project.

So many people sent encouraging words and notes along the way. And Bonita Markillie, a widow from Niles, Michigan, sent a donation to help with expenses related to the project.

Because of the amazing collaboration, the project was finished in five months, and every dollar that this book generates will go directly to support and bless Dena, Paige, and Parker. And not only that, they will have this book as a part of the legacy that Patrick left behind.

—Tim Stevens

Foreword

By Bob Johnson II

It has been said that if you set out to build a church, you probably won't build disciples, but if you set out to build disciples, you will probably build a church. From the day that Patrick McGoldrick became part of the ministry team at Cornerstone Baptist Church, he set out to build disciples. He constantly encouraged students to "follow hard after Christ" and gave much of his life to helping many of them do that. Along the way, there were a number of students who pursued vocational ministry in response to the influence of this man. They spent time with him. They ate with him. They were in his home. They ate with him. They went to events together. Did I say they ate with him? For Patrick, ministry was not a scheduled event as much as one life influencing another to lean upon and follow after Christ. But, what was it about Patrick that was so influential? And why did it seem that so many people knew this man?

Simply put, it was joy! This was a man who loved Christ, trusted Christ, and accepted Christ as Redeemer and King; he knew that he was loved by Christ, and it affected his entire life. He ministered to both students and senior saints with the same excitement. Patrick knew the gospel and was delighted to share it. His infectious laugh and engaging sense of humor put many people at ease, and yet he was able to speak to a person's heart and plead with someone when confrontation was needed. This heart endeared him to many, which meant that his wife, Dena, and children Paige and Parker had to share him with many as well. If shepherding junior high and high school students were not enough, Patrick led a weekly Bible study for our seasoned saints and became for them the son they loved. Then came ALS.

The initial symptoms were strange. Leg cramps—but he was jogging more than ever. Getting tired—well he was over forty-five. Sweating when he spoke in front of people. Really? Patrick, nervous in front of people? Patrick lived to be in front of people. What was this? It wasn't long until the diagnosis was confirmed, and it wasn't long again before the evidence of this disease began its cruel assault upon his body. Every week, another freedom was lost, another ability was taken away. The one who had served others then had to be served. Where was the joy then? Anybody can be happy on vacation. Where is the joy when you cannot walk, cannot talk, cannot chew, swallow, or stand? Where is your joy when your hand curls, your fingers do not work, and you cannot be left alone? ALS attacked every part of Patrick's body, but it never stole his joy. Joy is the result of realizing that Christ is all that you have and all that you need.

This book is a collection of sermons and writings from my friend Patrick McGoldrick. Some of the truths that are shared on these pages were spoken before hundreds of people but lived before an audience of One. To all of you who knew him, I hope that these pages will be the occasion for fresh grace and renewed perseverance. For those who did not, may you meet my dear friend around the throne of the Lamb. You will know him. He's the one with arms fully raised, fingers outstretched, both feet jumping, and laughing really loudly.

—Bob Johnson II
Senior Pastor, Cornerstone Baptist Church
Roseville, Michigan

Introduction

In November, 2011, a series of events started that made it the worst possible month. On Thanksgiving Day, Dena (my sister) pulled me aside and said, "You need to talk to Patrick. He's got some stuff going on, and it's really scary." Two days later, Patrick and I sat together at Big Apple Bagels on Garfield Road near his home in Clinton Township, Michigan. He talked about physical symptoms that had begun to surface a couple months prior. I had just spent a couple days with him during all of our family festivities, and hadn't noticed anything, although he did seem to be not quite as jovial.

He had difficulty laughing, he explained, and could no longer pronounce certain words. He tried to say "Google" for me, but he couldn't say it. He pointed to his arm and showed me how the muscles were quivering non-stop. He had been searching online, looking for possible diagnoses, but it kept coming back as either ALS or a brain tumor. If he had to choose between those two, he was hoping for a brain tumor. There were doctor visits and tests scheduled for the next week, so we agreed there was no reason to borrow trouble from the future.

A week later, on a Monday evening, my sister called to tell me the terrible news. The test results were 100% confirmed: Patrick had Amyotrophic Lateral Sclerosis (known as ALS or Lou Gehrig's disease). If he was average, the doctors said, he would live two to five years.

Two days later I drove to Taylor University to tell Heather her Uncle was dying, and then on to Detroit to hang with Patrick and Dena for the weekend. That Sunday morning he would stand up in front of his church, where he had served as the Youth Pastor for twelve years, and tell them that his days were numbered. Scores of students sat that morning in the front rows of the church, hearing for the first time that their youth pastor had a terminal illness. I still remember the looks on their faces.

I also remember that morning singing "Blessed Be the Name of the

1

Lord" and not being able to sing the part that says, "He gives and takes away . . ." It was just too hard. I was standing by my sister, next to their kids, Paige (18) and Parker (17), and was still in denial that any of this could be happening.

For the next year I drove to Detroit every few weeks to be with them and help where I could. We joined them in April when he preached his final sermon (see chapter 1); we gathered our family together in northern Michigan for a week in June; we watched people jump in to build ramps, widen doorways, renovate their bathroom, add stair railings, provide wheelchairs and chair lifts and more. The McGoldrick Family Fund was established and scores of people jumped in with donations, providing more than $50,000 to help with school bills and medical costs. It's been an amazing sight to behold.

If you want to help, visit:
www.wepay.com/donations/mcgoldrick

I'm not sure about the rest of my family, but I spent quite a bit of time in the stages of grief known as *denial* and *anger*. I really couldn't believe it was happening. I questioned why God would allow it. I still don't think He caused it (which is why I have a hard time with the song), but I know He is sovereign and could have stopped it. So for months, the question was, "Why?" Why will my sister not have a husband at such a young age? Why will Paige and Parker be without a dad in such an important time in their lives? And why is the disease progressing so much more quickly with Patrick than with others?

At some point in the last few months of his life, my focus shifted. I became overwhelmed with gratefulness. *I had a front-row seat to watch a man praise God until his dying breath.* He was a prisoner in his own wheelchair, yet did not curse God. He endured humiliating processes with the hospice nurse, yet he still smiled. He couldn't walk, scratch his nose, shoo a fly away, hold a pen or say a word. And yet he still praised God.

A few weeks before he died, while out of town, I wrote this note to my kids:

I know you haven't been this close to someone dying before, and it is a tragic thing. But I want you to know how rare it is that someone dies like Uncle Patrick is dying. Many (most?) people have a difficult time living. Life can be overwhelming and it is tough to do it with integrity and love. But as hard as living is, very few people die well. Some day in the next few weeks, Uncle Patrick will fall asleep and wake up in heaven. And he will be able to do so with a smile on his face and with no regrets. He didn't live a sinless life, but he lived a life of integrity. And even in his dying he is doing so with authenticity and vulnerability, while acknowledging his complete reliance on Jesus.

As hard as this time is on all of you, I'm so glad we don't live a thousand miles away, and you are able to experience it up close. He will be missed greatly, but we will all look back on his last days marveling at what a man of God he was all the way until the end.

Life is fragile, and we never know when our next encounter with someone will be our last, so live a life with no regrets, giving your all to everyone who you hold close and dear.

Yes, it was an honor to watch a man trust and praise God until his dying day. I can only pray that I will do the same.

Patrick's final blog entry was posted on December 5th—just twenty-one days before he would ultimately leave this world. He wrote:

I have accepted that this is the path God placed me on. I would not have chosen it. I don't like it. However, I am submitted that God in His Sovereignty, decided before all of time to give me a shorter life on earth. And if it keeps His name going forward and promotes His Kingdom, then who am I to question it? Who am I but God's servant placed here to bring Him glory? It's not supposed to be about me . . . it's about Him. If this promotes His Kingdom and Christ's name, then so be it.

Just like Joseph, Job, Daniel, Esther and many others throughout Scripture who ended up in circumstances that they did not ask for and they surely did not like, I daily must choose to focus on submitting to God's will, crying out for His grace and pointing to my Savior. After all, my sins are still my worst problem and Christ took care of that.

3

I asked Patrick last summer if it would be okay if we put some of his sermons in a book. I later learned that several people had been encouraging him for years to write a book. Now it would finally happen, and would become a part of his lasting legacy.

What follows are eleven sermons—delivered by Patrick over the final few years of his life—and selected by him for this book. I think you will be encouraged and inspired; you will laugh and you will cry; and you might even take a step toward Jesus. And ultimately, that is what Patrick would want.

—Tim Stevens
Author, Pastor, Brother-in-Law

Chapter 1

WHO DO YOU TRUST?
My Final Sermon

Imagine two different stools. One of them is rickety and barely standing. The legs are uneven and the seat is broken. With one look, you can tell it would never support you. The second stool is very secure. It looks well built. It is trustworthy. These represent two different ways of life. There are man's ways (stool #1) and then there are God's ways (stool #2). The question I have for you today is this: *Who do you trust?* Do you trust in the Redeemer? Do you trust in Christ? Or do you trust in man's ways?

My Story

To begin, I want to share a story with you about my life. For many, many years, my life was like a broken stool. My life was all about me, and I liked it that way. It was all about fun, friends, partying, and going to the beach.

I grew up in San Jose, California, so we went to the beach a lot. As a teen, my life was about drugs—even selling drugs. It was my life, and I did what I wanted to do. And I liked it. I really did. I thought, *This is the life!*

In August 1982, my parents' lives were falling apart. I was flunking out of school because I never went. It wasn't because I wasn't smart; I'm extremely intelligent! I just decided that I didn't want to go to

> My life was all about me, and I liked it that way.

school. My teachers didn't care, and my parents were at wits' end with me being a sixteen-year-old. They decided they were going to send me and my sister, Carla, to a place called Sharon, Pennsylvania.

From San Jose to Sharon; from palm trees to abandoned steel mills; from fun and friends to religious people I knew very little about; from maybe a frost or two each winter (I'd only seen snow one time in San Jose) to several feet of snow.

In San Jose, we didn't have humidity. When I got out of the airport in Pittsburgh and walked outside, I thought, *What in the world is this?* My whole body burst into a sweat. Now, my mom experienced this when she got a little older. One day she'd be walking along saying, "This is a nice day," and then two seconds later, she'd be dripping with sweat. I'd say, "What's wrong with you mom?" She'd just say, "Don't worry about it," and go on with life. But I'm pretty sure this California-to-Pennsylvania sweat was a different deal.

You get the picture: I was not too excited about moving from California to Pennsylvania, but that is where my cousins, Dave and Janet Searle, lived so off I went.

Janet was a Sunday school teacher. That was interesting to me, because I don't think I'd ever heard of Sunday school. (Saturday school was a whole different deal—I'd definitely heard of that!) Janet was also a choir director. I would see her up front moving her hands around and I'd think, "I can do that." Just seemed like an exercise class to me.

Janet was also a new mom of a one-year-old. So I moved across the country into this house with a one-year-old who poops and pees, and I'm cleaning it when it pukes. But as bad as that was, it wasn't the worst part.

Her husband, David, was a youth pastor. Who wants to move into a youth pastor's house? I never attended church when I was growing up. My parents were strictly nonreligious. Many of our friends went to church twice a year, on Easter and Christmas. My parents didn't want to be hypocritical, so they would say, "We are not people who only go to church on Easter and Christmas." So instead, we would just sleep in. And I liked that.

I got to Pennsylvania, and one of the first things Dave told me was, "Guess what, tomorrow we're going to church."

I said, "You're going to church, I'm staying here."

He said, "Well in my house, you're going with me to church." Then I found out that not only was he a youth pastor, he was the administrator of a small Christian school—the same school where I would be attending. I came from a high school of 5,000 kids. This school had 140 kids. Fantastic!

A Different Way to Live

Suddenly I was in this lifestyle with all these people who called themselves *Christians*. I called them religious fanatics. I knew nothing about Jesus other than He died, He rose again, and we did Easter egg hunts. That was about it.

These people were different. On the flight to Pennsylvania, I had won a bottle of wine. I was so happy. If my parents had been there and seen that I won a bottle of wine for them, my dad would have said, "I'm so proud of you boy, come on over here and let me give you a little hug and kiss." Not so with this new family. I got off the plane, greeted everyone, and Dave asked, "How was the flight?" I said, "Great, I won a bottle of wine!" Dave said, "We don't drink." He took the bottle and threw it in the garbage can.

So that was the world I was entering. How many of you would sign up for that? It was like basic training from hell. On my first night with the Searles, they must have been a little concerned about me, because they began to ask me questions that were foreign to me.

"Who have you placed your faith and trust in?"

I had no idea.

"Have you ever trusted in Christ as your savior?"

I didn't know what that meant.

"Are you saved?"

Saved from what?

All of these questions were foreign to me, and I was confused. But on that night and many nights during the next several weeks, all they talked about was the person of Jesus Christ. They said, "Patrick, if you died, where would you go?" I knew that answer—it was a no brainer. I said, "I'd go to hell! But I'd rather be in hell with my buddies than in heaven floating on clouds and playing a harp."

> Suddenly I was in this lifestyle with all these people who called themselves Christians. I called them religious fanatics.

David said, "You don't understand hell, do you?"

I said, "You don't understand heaven, do you?"

We battled and debated and argued for weeks, and my Irish, stubborn, pit bull–headed, arrogant, and prideful self kept noticing a difference between God's ways and my ways.

Who was I going to trust? David would say to me every night, "Tonight when you go to bed, I'm going to pray the Lord will give you no peace and that you won't sleep well until you give your life to Christ."

I would get up the next morning and tell David, "I slept like a baby!"

He would look at me and say, "I need to pray harder."

I would say, "David, you pray all you want."

I was with my cousins again two weeks ago, and we were recalling our time together. Janet said, "You were the only person in my life I ever wanted to kill."

"Likewise," I told her.

The Gospel Truth

Not only did they ask me questions about my life, they also opened up the Bible. Go figure, I didn't have one. I had all my rock tapes and Coors Light beer bottles and Budweiser hats but no Bible. David and Janet found this big Bible and opened it up and began to read for me from Romans:

As it is written: "There is no one righteous, not even one; there is no one who understands, no one who seeks God. All have turned away, they have together become worthless; there is no one who does good, not even one." (Romans 3:10–12)

They said to me, "This is you, Patrick."

"Now hold on there a little bit. I've done some pretty good things in my life before," I said. "Those are murderers and bad people and rapists, that's who they're describing."

"Their mouths are full of cursing and bitterness. Their feet are swift to shed blood; ruin and misery mark their ways, and the way of peace they do not know. There is no fear of God before their eyes." (Romans 3:14–18)

They graciously said to me, "Patrick, this a picture of your heart. This is who you are without Christ." And I had to be honest: When looking at my cousins' lives compared to mine, there was a huge difference.

Then they showed me Romans 3:23:

For all have sinned and fall short of the glory of God.

I knew I did some bad things. However, I would always open the door for old people, I was always gracious, and if there was litter to be picked up, I would do it. I would help people, but still they said, "No, Patrick, it's more than that. You are spiritually dead. You have no relationship with Jesus Christ." And they said, "You are on your way to hell, and hell is real."

David kept going, "I'm not here to scare you, I'm here to tell you the truth. There is heaven and there is hell, and there is nothing in between. You're going to one or the other." At some point, I realized they used the word "hell" more than my parents did (which I didn't think possible). But I hated it, because the more they talked, the more I knew they were describing me.

I didn't like when people rebuked me or told me I was wrong. I was the one to tell others they were wrong. Don't get in my face.

But time and again I would hear their loving rebuke. They began to share how Jesus Christ changed their lives, and how they trusted in faith and Christ alone. They told me about the Messiah being prophesied in the Old Testament, then born of a virgin and living a sinless life. Try and live a sinless day, or hour, or minute. Jesus did that. He lived a sinless, pure life, and He went to the cross and gave Himself for our sins.

They said, "Patrick, Christ died for you, do you understand that?" Well intellectually, yes, I understood. But I began to question what it would mean if I trusted Christ in my heart and my life. I wasn't sure I wanted to change yet. They didn't stop coming at me. David said, "Patrick, when Christ died, He did not remain dead. Do you know what He did?"

I knew the answer: "He rose again on the third day, right?" Nailed it. But it was more than that. David said, "He rose again on the third day. He defeated death. Jesus Christ conquered death. Try that! Christ conquered death and is now seated at the right hand of God."

Then they began to share more good news about Christ and what He has done.

You see, at just the right time, when we were still powerless, Christ died for the ungodly. Very rarely will anyone die for a righteous person, though for a good person someone might possibly dare to die. But God demonstrates his own love for us in this: While we were still sinners, Christ died for us. (Romans 5:6–8)

Think about that. Christ died for ungodly people. Not for godly people, not for kind people, not for gracious people—He died for the ungodly. Who are the ungodly? We are.

If you declare with your mouth, "Jesus is Lord," and believe in your heart that God raised him from the dead, you will be saved. (Romans 10:9)

What a powerful verse. This is one of those verses that really grabbed a hold of my heart. I didn't really know what "saved" meant. But I was beginning to understand that if I declared with my mouth that Jesus Christ is Lord and believed in my heart that God raised Him from the dead—I could go from an old way of life (sitting on a rickety stool) to a new way of life (trusting in God).

Then he read for me Ephesians 2:8–9:

For it is by grace you have been saved, through faith . . .

Faith. It is a faith in what Christ has done. He went to the cross and finished what He was called to do.

. . . and this is not from yourselves, it is the gift of God—not by works, so that no one can boast.

I thought if there was any way of me getting to heaven it was going to be because I was friendly enough or good enough. But the Bible says there is no other way to get to heaven than through the person of Jesus Christ. No other way. No church, no religious figure, not even a good deed. You cannot earn your way to heaven. You cannot do anything apart from accepting what Christ has done in your life for forgiveness of sin.

Decision Time

So I was hearing all of this stuff, and the truth was that I knew my life was a mess on the outside. I mean, it's pretty tough to flunk physical education when you're a jock. I took the easiest English class just to get a passing grade. Yeah, I was a mess on the outside.

But more importantly, I began to realize my heart was also a mess. There was something that was missing. I thought the good life was about *me,* and now I was being told the good news of Jesus was for me.

My family was totally different from what I was experiencing. My sister and I grew up in a home that was somewhat rough. There was fear, alcoholism, divorce, and more. You name it, they did it. It was a disaster.

But my Pennsylvania family was different. They were caring and compassionate. They were dirt poor, and yet they never complained. Somehow, we always had food. They loved God, and I began to notice the difference between them and myself. It was during that time when these two ways of life—man's ways and God's ways—began to collide. And it wasn't a little fender bender, it was a massive collision. Yet I would fight and argue with God and with my cousins. It was a battle over who I trusted. Did I trust in God's way or in man's ways?

(Side note: I recommend you vote God every time. Wave that white flag of surrender. You can do whatever you want, but you're going to lose the battle when it comes to God.)

I knew the path I was on was not good, and something happened about three weeks after I arrived. Night after night, I sat through them telling me about the story of Christ; I went to church week after week; I experienced people singing and being way too nice; and I kept hearing the preaching of the Word.

One Sunday morning the pastor said, "How many of you want to trust Christ as the Lord of your life?" So I put my hand up, because I realized I didn't want that life anymore. He asked me to come forward, and my best friend Matt said, "Hey I'll go down there with you." We walked to the front, and a gentleman met me. He took me into a room, read Romans 3, and made sure I understood what Christ did for me. I'll tell you what: I could have explained it to him better than he explained it to me.

It was that morning, September 5, 1982, that I prayed and placed my faith and trust in Jesus Christ and Him alone. God saved me that day. He changed my life, and I walked out of that office saying, "Phew, man. Something is different."

> I began to realize my heart was also a mess. There was something that was missing.

There was still a battle to go back to that way of life. But I was no longer with any of my druggie or party friends. Now I was with Matt, my cousins, and other guys who loved God; and they discipled me and encouraged me. Looking back, I believe that if God had not saved me, I'd be in jail or dead right now. But He did save me.

Trust in the Lord

I just told you the story of how I came to faith in Christ. A question I have for each of you is this: *Do you trust Christ every day?* You might call yourself a follower of Jesus Christ, but when things get difficult in your life, do you go back to your own ways, or do you follow God's ways? That's my challenge today.

Take your Bible and turn to the book of Proverbs. Salvation isn't only for eternity, it is for everyday life. Proverbs 3:5–6 is familiar to a lot of us:

Trust in the Lord with all your heart and lean not on your own understanding; in all your ways submit to him, and he will make your paths straight.

Trust in the Lord with how much of your heart? Trust in the Lord with *all* your heart. Now, is this a command or a suggestion? It is a command. This is talking about everything. Trust in God. Trust in the Lord with all your heart—everything in your life. Trust in Him.

Trust is contrary to us. A lot of us are skeptics. We've been burned, and we do not like to trust people. But when we don't trust, what do we do? We doubt. And when we doubt God, it's ugly. It is destructive. It minimizes God. Doubt leads to poor decisions. Doubt is like cancer. It eats everything that is good. Hear me: This is real. This is real because when we doubt what God says or what He does, we minimize God to nothing. By our lack of trust, we are saying, "My ways and God's ways are the same."

In this passage, Solomon is saying, "No, trust in the Lord with all of your heart, because when you lean on your own understanding, it leads to destruction."

There is an example of doubt that we see in the Scriptures in the book of Matthew. The disciples are in a boat in the Sea of Galilee and Jesus is not with them. A storm comes, and suddenly Christ goes out walking on the water.

"Lord, if it's you," Peter replied, "tell me to come to you on the water." "Come," he said. Then Peter got down out of the boat, walked on the water and came toward Jesus. But when he saw the wind, he was afraid and, beginning to sink, cried out, "Lord, save me!" (Matthew 14:28–30)

Interesting. Peter gets out of the boat. I love Peter. I think I'm a little bit like Peter other than I probably would have gone under a lot sooner. Peter gets out there on the water, and where does his focus go? It goes off of Christ, onto the wind, and onto the waves. What does Christ ask him? He asks, "Why do you doubt? Why didn't you trust Me, don't you know who I am? My promises are true. My Word is true. Peter, you can trust Me even if a great tsunami comes. You can put your trust in Me."

But what does Peter do? He begins to see other things around him. Proverbs 3:5–6 says to trust in the Lord with all your heart. Don't lean on your own understanding.

Another example of doubt is in the very first chapter of James, where James is talking about trials. Have you ever had a trial in your life or perhaps a time where you went through something difficult? James says, "If you would desire wisdom, ask of God and he'll give it you liberally" (James 1:5).

(We don't like using the word "liberal" in a Baptist church—ha!)

James was saying, "God will give it to you liberally, but you cannot ask and doubt." James describes this as a person who is like a wave in the wind. He's tossed up and down; he's tossed to the side. He has no direction in his life. Later in the verse, he says that person will not receive wisdom. He is double-minded and unstable. Beautiful description. "How would you describe yourself, Patrick?" Well, I have no wisdom, I'm double-minded, and I'm unstable." Not a way you want to be described. Let me tell you, nothing good comes from doubt. It takes your focus off of Christ and places it on yourself.

But there is a second phrase in Proverbs 3:5–6. It says, "And lean not on your own understanding." Boy that's a tough one. We are such self-sufficient people. "I can fix it. Don't worry about it, honey, this is taken care of. You don't have to worry about anything, I've got this ironed out." Here's the thing. We're not talking about fixing the lawn mower or an iPod, iPad, iShelf, or iWhatever thing you might have that breaks down. We're talking about life. Don't lean on your own understanding.

John MacArthur makes this statement: "When we lean on our own understanding, we minimize God." When I lean on my own understanding, I am saying to God, "I don't need You."

There are things that we cannot fix. I can't fix ALS, so what do I do? I find comfort in the fact that I don't have to lean on my own understanding. I want to follow what Solomon says: "Trust in God with your heart." He gives such a peace, such a hope, and such a joy.

Solomon makes this statement in Proverbs 3:6: " . . . in all your ways acknowledge Him and He will make your paths straight." He is saying, "It isn't about a recognition of God but an intimate knowledge of God." It's not just a cool verse. No, it is about who God is. If I trust God rather than leaning on my own understanding—then my path will be like the difference driving from Michigan on Interstate 75 to Ohio: "Ahhhh, pothole city to smooth roads."

> I find comfort in the fact that I don't have to lean on my own understanding.

It doesn't mean everything will go our way. The verse doesn't mean that everything will turn out right. What it does mean is that God is the One who is in control, not man. Allow God to direct; don't lean on yourself; in all your ways, acknowledge who He is. He will direct you. That gives comfort and peace.

The Sovereignty of God

How can God promise this? I mean, that's a pretty big promise.

Sometimes we forget that He is God and we are not, and His promises are always fulfilled. A term that we don't use a lot in our country is the term *sovereign* or *sovereignty*. It is talking about the sovereignty of God, meaning that God is in complete control. John Piper makes this statement: "Do you want your heart comforted? Understand the sovereignty of God. If you want to give hope to someone, understand the sovereignty of God."

He is the one who is in control. God is not up in heaven going, "Oops. Oh man, this person has cancer. I didn't know about that." No. He is sovereign. He is in control. He allows things to take place for reasons that at times we just don't understand. And that's okay. His ways are not my ways, and thankfully my ways are not His ways.

We see one example of the sovereignty of God (God being in control) in the life of Joseph. I have the privilege of teaching some adults in a Wednesday morning Bible study, and we are going through the life of Joseph right now. Wow, you talk about a guy who went through the ringer, yet God was in control the entire time. Let me set up Joseph's life for you a little bit.

Joseph was one of twelve brothers. He was the favorite son of his father, Jacob, and his brothers hated him. Joseph had a dream one night that his family would bow down to him. So what did he do? He went and told his family. Not a smart move. It's like my sister coming and saying to me, "Hey, one of these days you're going to bow down to me." Uh, I don't think so. If you have that dream, keep it to yourself. Don't tweet it; don't put it on Facebook.

Anyway, they found out they didn't like his dream, so what did they do? They stripped him of his clothes and sold him to some strangers. He landed up in Egypt as a slave. They went back and they told their father, "Your son was killed by a wild animal." Now, first of all, they hated him—a sin. Second, they sold him—also a sin. Third, they went to their father and lied by saying he was attacked by an animal.

Joseph was sold off into slavery, but over time God prospered him. He became second in command to Potiphar. Potiphar was the big dog. He ran important things, and Potiphar's wife looked at Joseph and said, "I like you." She made a move on him. What did Joseph do? He ran away from the temptation.

She tried to seduce him again, and he boldly got in her face and said, "I will not sin against my God, and I will not sin against my master." And he took off and ran out of the house. About that time in the story, we all stand up and applaud him. "Go Joseph!"

Something would obviously come out of this that was good for Joseph. Yeah, jail time. Potiphar's wife went back and told her husband, "He tried to seduce me." And he went back to jail.

It looked like this guy could not get a break. But the hand of God was always working through Joseph's life. He was in prison after being falsely accused but soon found favor with the captain. Everywhere he went, people really appreciated him. I believe it was because of his relationship with God. Remember, God was still in control.

While in prison, two of his prison buddies had dreams: the cupbearer and the baker. Joseph interpreted the dreams. To the cupbearer he said, "You're going to live and will be serving Pharaoh very soon. So do me a favor, and when you get out of here, remember me."

To the baker he said, "You're gonna die." And he died.

So what did the cupbearer do when he got out of prison? Nothing. He forgot his promise to Joseph. So Joseph spent two more years in prison. What had he done wrong? Nothing. But God was in control.

Then we are told that Pharaoh, the leader of Egypt, had a dream. Ding, Ding, Ding. The cupbearer said, "Hey, I remember a guy. He can interpret dreams." So Pharaoh found Joseph, and he was able to interpret his dream. Pharaoh saw the character of Joseph and put him in charge. He was like the vice president for Pharaoh. His job? "Do what you need to do, help the people."

So along came his brothers. They didn't realize Joseph was now the vice president. What would you do if you were Joseph? I think I might beat my brothers up a bit, teach them a lesson. Not Joseph. His brothers found out who he was, and they were terrified that they would be killed:

16

But Joseph said to them, "Don't be afraid. Am I in the place of God? You intended to harm me, but God intended it for good to accomplish what is now being done, the saving of many lives." (Genesis 50:19–20)

Joseph knew that God intended all of the pain and suffering for good.

How do you make sense of that in your mind? The hand of God was involved every step of the way in the life of Joseph. Did he have to go through difficult times? Definitely, but it was part of His timing. God can even use the sin of people to accomplish His purpose, because He is in control. He is the One who is on the throne.

> Joseph knew that God intended all of the pain and suffering for good.

Because of Proverbs 3:5–6, we can say, "God, we trust You because You are sovereign, and You are good, and Your purposes are good."

A Lesson from Jonah

Those of you who have been at Cornerstone Baptist for a while know that I preached through the book of Jonah (see these messages later in this book). I'm sure you remember every detail of my scintillating messages!

Jonah's life is another example of the sovereignty of God, even over Jonah's rebellion. God says to Jonah, "Go to Nineveh and preach."

Jonah says, "No thank you. I'm not going there, I'm not going to preach that." Now how did that work out for Jonah? Not very well. Jonah's response was, "I'm out of here, I want nothing to do with it."

He runs from God by jumping on a ship. I love the idea that you run from God. Anytime you think, *I'm gonna play hide-and-seek with God,* it's not going to work. He always knows where you are. From the highest of heights to the lowest of lows, He is there. You can't play hide-and-seek with an omnipresent God. He's everywhere.

But Jonah thought he could. He didn't want to do what God asked, he didn't want to go to Nineveh to preach.

Then the Lord sent a great wind on the sea, and such a violent storm arose that the ship threatened to break up. (Jonah 4:1)

It was a pretty big storm, folks, to the point that the ship was ready to break up. Now the Hebrew language says God hurled a storm at them. We're not talking old man, slow-pitch softball. We're talking a Justin Verlander 100 mph fastball. God threw it at them. Who was in control here? The Lord sent the wind and the violent storm, but the interesting thing we learn is that everyone on the ship was afraid for their lives except for one person: Jonah. He was so rebellious. He still wasn't going to follow God.

The crew threw him in the water, and what did God do?

Now the Lord provided a huge fish to swallow Jonah, and Jonah was in the belly of the fish three days and three nights. (Jonah 4:17)

It was the Lord who produced the wind. It was the Lord who caused the storm. It was the Lord who provided the fish. God was trying to get Jonah's attention, but Jonah was still rebelling.

God did all of this to get Jonah's attention. He was in control all along the way: from the fish, to dry ground, to preaching, to a great revival in Nineveh where everyone repented. You would think by then Jonah would be celebrating and saying, "Wow, look at all of these people who have turned away from sin to follow God!"

Not Jonah. He wasn't celebrating. He was angry with God. He threw himself a pity party.

Watch what happened next:

Then the Lord God provided a leafy plant and made it grow up over Jonah to give shade for his head to ease his discomfort, and Jonah was very happy about the plant. But at dawn the next day God provided a worm, which chewed the plant so that it withered. (Jonah 4:6–7)

Who was in control of the story? The Lord was. God will use even the rebellious heart of people to accomplish His purpose. That's right, He can use ungodly people. We see in the book of Isaiah where He uses ungodly people to get the attention of His people. God uses all different means, from the storm to the fish to the revival. From plants to a worm, God is sovereign over everything. God has never been surprised.

In the book of Isaiah, the writer makes this statement: "In the year that King Uzziah died, I saw the Lord seated on His throne" (Isaiah 1:6).

Where is the King supposed to be seated? On His throne. Isaiah didn't say, "In the year that King Uzziah died, I looked up and saw the Lord, and He was pacing because He didn't know what to do because He didn't realize someone died." It doesn't say He formed a committee to figure out what to do. Where is the King seated? On the throne. Where is the King supposed to be seated? On the throne. You know why? He is in control.

My Struggle with ALS

So who do you trust in everyday life? Who have you placed your faith in? Yourself? It is man's ways that lead to destruction. Following your own way does not lead to hope, glory, peace, or joy.

Or have you placed your faith and your trust in Jesus Christ? Friends, that is the hope that we have. You might not understand what I'm saying. That is why we have the Bible. It has the answers for all your questions. The hero of the Bible is our Savior, Jesus Christ, and we rest in Him.

I've been diagnosed with ALS, and there is no cure for it. Ultimately, it will take my life. People will say, "That's not fair." They don't understand the sovereignty of God. To be honest, fairness is hell. I am finite, God is infinite, and I cannot pretend to understand why.

Do I struggle with it? Oh yeah, every day; even every few minutes. Do I get discouraged? Sure. Do I question why? Yeah.

Do I fear death? No. No way. Bring it on! Here is the reason I don't fear death. I'm a follower of Jesus Christ. God has called me to walk this road, and I know that I am not alone. I have family, friends, you, but more importantly—I have my Savior.

> Do I fear death? No. No way. Bring it on! Here is the reason I don't fear death. I'm a follower of Jesus Christ.

This is a statement that Pastor Bob Johnson gave me, and it is so powerful that I want you to hear it. But I do not want you to feel sorry for me. He said, "My shorter road with Christ is infinitely greater than a longer road without Christ." My short road with Christ is greater than a longer road without Christ. So do not pity me. I pity those who live for it all yet lose it all.

Again, my shorter road with Christ is infinitely greater than a longer road without Christ. To God be the glory. Amen.

April 22, 2012
Cornerstone Baptist Church
Watch this sermon online at https://vimeo.com/41122112

Chapter 2

WHERE IS YOUR FOCUS?
Colossians 3—Part I

In 1961, Arnold Palmer, one of the greatest golfers in the world, was at the Masters golf tournament. He was on the 18th and last hole, had a one-stroke lead, and all he had to do was finish well. He got up to the tee, stepped up to the ball, completely focused on what he needed to do. As he swung, the ball sailed down the middle of the fairway. It didn't go into the trees, it didn't hit someone in the gallery, it went straight down the middle—a perfect shot. As he walked to his second shot, an old friend motioned for Arnold to come over. As Arnold approached, his friend stuck out his hand and said, "Congratulations on winning the Masters." Arnold Palmer put his hand out, shook it, and said, "Thank you."

At that point, Arnold completely lost focus of what he needed to do. He came up to his second shot thinking about that infamous green jacket, thinking about finishing well, and thinking about getting out of there.

All he needed to do to win the Masters Tournament was hit the ball in the hole in three strokes. He stepped up, thinking about that green jacket, took the second shot, and stuck it directly in the sand trap. His third shot went over the green far past the hole, and his fourth shot was a terrible putt that landed fifteen feet from the hole. The commentators exclaimed, "What is happening? What has happened?" Arnold Palmer had lost the Masters Tournament.

In later interviews, Arnold said, "The reason I lost the Masters was that I lost my focus. What I was supposed to do, I did not do. What I wasn't supposed to do, I did."

Where Is Our Focus?

The book of Colossians was written by the apostle Paul to the church in Colossae. Paul desired for them to grow and to be challenged, but there were a lot of false things that were being taught, many of which focused on man-made religion and traditions. The book of Colossians can basically be summarized as this: "Christ is supreme. He is over all." When you look at the first two chapters of the book of Colossians, you will notice Paul, time and time and time again, reiterates that Christ is supreme: supreme over the angels, and supreme in the fact that Christ was a part of the creation process. Chapters three and four then instruct the church in Colossae how they are to live in light of Christ's supremacy. The question for us today is the same: *Where is our focus?* Do we focus on Christ being over all? Colossians 3:1–4 says:

> *Since you have been raised with Christ, set your hearts on things above where Christ is seated at the right hand of God. Set your minds on things above not on earthly things, for you died and your life is now hidden with Christ in God. When Christ, who is your life, appears, then you also appear with him in Glory.*

Raised with Christ

Look at verse 1 again: "Since you have been raised with Christ, set your hearts on things above where Christ is seated at the right hand of God." *Since you've been raised with Christ.* What comes to your mind when you think of that? Paul is saying that since you've been raised with Christ, you are alive in Jesus Christ! It is a beautiful terminology. Galatians 2:20 says this: "I have been crucified with Christ and it is no longer I who live, but it is Christ who lives in me and the life I now live in the flesh I live by the flesh and the Son of God who loved me and delivered himself up for me."

Focusing Our Hearts

Paul says to "set your hearts on things above." Now this word *set* really means "seek." Many of you have played hide-and-seek before. There is one goal for the hider: Don't be found. And there is one goal for the seeker: Find the person who doesn't want to be found. Paul is saying, "Listen, I want you to set your hearts on things above."

I tend to misplace things every once in a while, either my keys or my wallet or my cell phone. My cell phone is usually the easiest to find because I can just call it. But it's a different story when I misplace my wallet. I will look in my car under the seat, in the glove box, and in the trunk. Then I will go into the house and look everywhere I can think it may be. I think, *What was the last pair of pants that I wore? What was the last jacket I wore?* Finally, I will come in and blame my kids, because that is why we have children. Obviously, they must have taken it. Then I go back and look in the pants and the jacket once more. And you know what I do next? I go back out to the car and just reverse the whole ugly cycle over and over, because I want to find my wallet. That is the intensity Paul is trying to communicate: Set your hearts—your affections—on things above.

What Paul is saying here is not a suggestion. He is not saying, "I've got a great idea. On Sundays when you're in church, that is like dress rehearsal. When you're in church on Sunday, try to focus your attention on things above. As for Monday, Tuesday, Wednesday, Thursday, Friday, and Saturday . . . not so much." This is a *command*, not a suggestion. It is not simply a command to do once, it is continual action. As followers of Jesus Christ, since you have been raised with Christ, all your affections and thoughts should be focused on things that are above, all the time. Is that hard to do? It is very difficult!

> All your affections and thoughts should be focused on things that are above, all the time.

Jesus put it this way in Matthew 6:33: "Seek first His kingdom and His righteousness." Jesus uses the same terminology—you are to be seeking after those things. Again, it is not for a period of time, it is not just during a vacation or during church. It is all the time.

Christ Is Seated

Paul goes on a little further in verse 1 and describes *where* we are to set our hearts. He says we are to set our hearts on things above, "where Christ is seated at the right hand of God." Think of that, Christ is *seated*. He is not up in heaven at the right hand of God going, "Oh man, what am I going to do?" He is not nervously pacing, He is not biting his nails, and He is not wondering what is going to happen next. Where is Christ? He is seated. Do you know why? Because He is in control. He is on the throne.

Isaiah 6 describes God as "high and lifted up, seated on his throne." Why is God seated on His throne? It is because God is in complete control. So Paul is saying, "Do not take your hearts and affections and think on things that are just up in heaven somewhere, but think on things where Christ is seated, at the right hand of God."

The question we have to ask is, *Where do I want my focus to be?* It is so easy for our focus to be here and for our affections to be drawn here because we can see what is here on Earth. It is so easy for our affections to be drawn to relationships or friendships or things that we enjoy doing because we are a part of those things here and now. Paul is saying to set it on things above where Christ is seated—at the right hand of God! Is there a better place for us to focus our attention? No!

At Pentecost, Peter told the crowd that Christ had been exalted to the right hand of God (Acts 5:31). Later in the same book, as Stephen was being killed, he cried out, "Behold I see the heavens opened up and the Son of man standing at the right hand of God" (Acts 7:56). Where is Christ? He's at the right hand of God. Paul describes it a little further in Romans 8:34 by telling us Christ is the One who is at the right hand of God. And what does He do at the right hand of God? He intercedes for you and for me. Ephesians 1:20 says, "God raised Him from the dead and seated him at His right hand in the heavenly places."

Where is Christ? He is seated; He is seated at the right hand of God, and He intercedes for us. So then, where should our affections be drawn? Where should our focus be? It needs to be on those things where Christ is, where He is seated, right next to God His father.

Don't Trust Your Heart

Now, why would Paul say, "Have your affections set on things above"? It is because Paul understands the heart. Jeremiah 17:9 says, "The heart is deceitful above all things and beyond cure—who can know it?" When you look at Scripture, you can see a lot of different people who tried to do certain things. You look at their lives and realize that they crashed and burned. Adam and Eve, in their hearts, wanted to be like God. David's heart led him to adultery and to murder. Peter's heart led him to deny Christ. Judas' heart led him to betray Christ.

You and I are one heart decision away from destroying our lives. Let me say that again, and I will make it personal: I am one heart decision away from destroying my entire life. Jeremiah says that the heart is wicked. It is deceitful. There is no reason why we should ever want to trust our hearts. If we understand the wickedness of our hearts, we will realize our focus needs to be on those things that are above, where Christ is seated at the right hand of God.

Paul gives us some insight in Romans 7:15 that can be summarized as this: "I do the things I don't want to do, and I don't do the things that I should do." You see, there is a battle for my heart, and there is a battle for your heart. There is a battle for my affections, and there is a battle for your affections. Where is your focus when it comes to your affections? Is it on things here on earth, or is it where Christ is seated, at the right hand of God? There's not a better place that my affections need to be than on Jesus Christ, seated at the right hand of the Father.

Focusing Our Minds

Paul then moves on in verse 2 of Colossians 3 to focusing our minds. He says, "Set your minds on things above, not on earthly things." Now the term *set* here does not mean "seek." It means "think." Think through, think about, and set your mind on things above, not on earthly things. The concentration here is still very important. The Colossians were being led astray by mysterious philosophies and different theologies, and Paul wanted them to understand they needed to first set their affections on where Christ is seated at the right hand of God and then *think* about those things that are above.

Our minds wander easily—no question about it. In Paul's day there were distractions just like there are now. Paul is saying, "Listen! You need to set your minds. You need to think on things that are above, on things that are pure. Set your minds on things above, not on earthly things."

There are a lot of religions out there that say, "Empty your mind. Sit down, close your eyes. Relax, breathe, and empty your mind." It is interesting because when I look in Scripture I don't see any place that it says I am to empty my mind. It is the exact opposite. I need to fill my mind. In Romans 12:2, Paul makes the statement, "Do not be conformed to the pattern of this world but be transformed by the renewing of your minds." Again, in Philippians 4:8, Paul says, "Finally brothers, whatever is true, whatever is noble, pure, lovely, admirable, if anything is excellent or praiseworthy, think on these things." He doesn't tell us to get rid of those things; rather, we are to think on them. So we are to set our minds on what is true, on what is noble, right, pure and lovely.

Paul shows a contrast here. He knows we are distracted. Theological commentator J. B. Lightfoot makes this statement: "You must not only seek heaven, you must *think* heaven." What it comes down to is taking the Scriptures and filling our minds with it so that when we are in a situation where we are tempted to do what is wrong, the first thing that comes to our mind is Scripture! It is hard! It takes discipline and commitment to the Scriptures. Currently, I am memorizing 1 Corinthians 13. It isn't easy. It is a battle to memorize it. But harder than that, it is a battle to live it out. I find, though, the more I absorb Scripture, and the more I let it go through every part of my brain, every part of my heart, it is at that time that what is going to come out of me will be things that are pure, noble, and right. I must fill my mind with Scripture.

The author of Hebrews helps us out a little here. Hebrews 12:2 says, "Let us fix our eyes on Jesus." This term *fix* is not a glance. Then he describes Christ as the author and perfector of our faith. He is the One who wrote it, and He is the One who has perfected it. Is there a better person who I need to fix my eyes on? No. It is so easy to get distracted.

I was raised with Christ on September 5, 1982. When Christ saved me, my old nature did not take on a cosmetic makeover or a superficial change. No, it was put to death. *Put to death.* Therefore, as a follower of Christ, I am alive to Christ, dead to sin. Where do my affections need to be? They need to be fixed on Jesus Christ and on those things that are above. Because of the death and resurrection of Christ, I am secure in Him. He is the author, and He is the perfector of my faith.

Hidden with Christ in God

Another amazing thing about this passage is that (in verse 3) Paul says that nothing can ever separate us from who Jesus Christ is. Since we have died with Christ, our life is now hidden with Christ in God and eternally secure. You may have seen the Allstate commercial, where they make the statement, "You're in good hands." Unlike temporary, earthly insurance, I know I am safely in the hands of God because it says, " . . . for you died." My old nature is dead. Patrick's life as a follower of Christ is now hidden with Christ in God. What a beautiful picture!

> I am secure in Him. He is the author, and He is the perfector of my faith.

Christ Is Our Life

Paul is telling them to set their hearts and minds on things above, because they are dead to their sins and dead people do not act that way. How should they act? A follower of Christ should say, "I am setting my heart and mind on things above."

Paul continues in verse 4: "When Christ who is your life appears, then you also will appear with him in glory." In the book of John, you see Christ describing Himself as *the way, the truth, and the life.* When Christ is your life, what else do you need? You have a Savior, Christ, who is your life! Yet we will make statements like, "I live for this, I live for that, I live to go here, and I live to be a part of this," but nothing will ever be like Christ, who is your life and my life. He is everything I need to place my faith, my hope, and my trust in.

When Christ, who is your life, appears, then you also will appear with Him in glory. That is why our focus needs to be on Christ and our lives need to be centered on Him. Christ, not this world, needs to be the center of the believer's universe, because our future is with Christ in glory. He has allowed us to be a part of this wretched world to lead, to shepherd, to help, to give counsel and to point people to who He is. I look forward to that day in glory! I look forward to the light being completely different. I look forward to the singing with the millions and millions of saints who are in Christ, coming together in glory.

Christ, Christ, Christ, Christ

"Christ" is used four times in Colossians 3:1–4:

> *Since you have been raised with Christ, set your hearts on things above where Christ is seated at the right hand of God. Set your minds on things above not on earthly things, for you died and your life is now hidden with Christ in God. When Christ, who is your life, appears, then you also appear with him in Glory.*

Do you think Paul is trying to get a message across? Today, when we have an important message to get across, we usually yell. The Hebrews, however, would use a word once if it was important, twice if it was *really* important, and three times it was *really, really, really* important. If you were a Hebrew child running around during Old Testament times and your mother or father said to you, "Come over here, come over here, come over here," you knew that you better get over there! Now we just say, "GET OVER HERE!" Therefore, when Paul, in four verses, is saying "Christ, Christ, Christ, Christ," do you think he's trying to get a point across? I do.

Is Our Focus on Christ?

The question I have for us today is this: *Where is our focus?* Is it where Christ is seated, at the right hand of God the Father? Is my mind focused on things above and not on things that are on Earth, not on these temporary things? Not everything is bad, but the question is: *Is it the best? Where is my focus?*

Ken Davis is a Christian comedian and an avid archer. He is so good at archery, he can take his bow and his arrow, aim for the target, and hit the bull's-eye. What's more, he can take a second arrow, release it, and split the first arrow that he already shot into the target. Basically, the guy is a really good shot!

Years ago, Ken Davis was up in a tree stand hunting deer. From a distance, he said he saw "a monster trophy buck walking toward me. I was so excited about it I had to calm myself down and had to start breathing normally again." The buck continued to get closer, and he said, "The closer it got, the bigger that rack got, and all I could think was, 'I cannot wait to shoot this thing, kill it, and mount it in my living room.'"

As Ken Davis got up to take his shot, the deer came closer and closer and was in perfect position. As he excitedly pulled back the arrow, he released and the arrow hit the deer . . . on the rack. He said, "I was so focused on the rack, I forgot about where to shoot him, and I hit the rack. The arrow went up in the sky, and the deer took off."

I love that story, probably because I have never shot a deer with a bow. But think about this: Ken Davis can split another arrow already on the target, so you would think that he would be able to take an arrow and stick it through that deer where it needed to be stuck. Where was his focus? It was on the wrong thing, it was on the rack.

Where is your focus? Is it seated on things above? Is your heart set on things above, where Christ is seated, at the right hand of God? Is your mind thinking things that are above and not earthly things? Is that difficult to do? Yes it is. But it is not a suggestion, it is a command. Let us strive to follow these commands in Colossians 3.

Closing Prayer

Father, thank You for saving us. Thank You that, since we have been raised with Christ, Your desire, Lord, is for our affections to be fixed on Jesus where He is seated at your right hand. Your desire, Father, is for us to take our minds and think about You, not on these earthly things because we are so easily distracted. Lord, I pray that that would be our heart's desire and that we would ask the question, "Where is our focus?" Is it on You where it needs to be? Or is it on everything else? Thank you, Father, for your Son who came to this world and walked on this earth and gave His life for us so that we could be raised with Jesus Christ. May our affections and our minds be set upon You and on what You desire for us to do. We pray this all in the wonderful name of Jesus Christ, who is seated at the right hand of God, who intercedes for us. Amen.

April 15, 2007
Cornerstone Baptist Church

Chapter 3

ARE YOU STILL PLAYING WITH FIRE?
Colossians 3—Part II

In Colossians 3, Paul wrote to a group of believers called the Colossians. There was a lot of mysterious teaching going on in the Colossian church, and, in chapters 1 and 2, Paul sets a great theological foundation: Christ is supreme over all. He then continues in chapter 3, telling them that their hearts and minds need to be focused and set on things above and not on earthly things. When I read Colossians 3, I ask myself this question: *How often do I need to refocus?* If you are a hunter, you take binoculars, go out and look for that particular animal that you are going to shoot, and you have to move the binoculars in such a way that you have clear focus. Some of you put on glasses before you start reading so that you can actually see. That is called refocusing, and in Colossians 3, Paul says that we need to refocus some things.

Put Sin to Death

He also says that we need to put to death and kill certain things—destroy them. Do not allow them to breathe any breath; do not allow them to have any life in them. We do not like talking about death; we sorrow over death. When someone that we love passes away, we cry. If he or she is a follower of Christ, we cry, yet we rejoice. It is that awkwardness of knowing that person is in the presence of the Lord yet missing the loved one terribly. We do not sell death insurance, we sell *life* insurance. I have never had someone say, "I have a great death insurance policy for you." It used to be called death insurance, but people did not like the name of it. In all actuality, we are buying death insurance; we pay a premium so that, when we die, someone will get some money for our death.

In this passage, Paul is talking about putting to death certain things in our lives. He writes:

> *Put to death therefore whatever belongs to your earthly nature. Sexual immorality, impurity, lust, evil desires, and greed, which is idolatry. Because of these, the wrath of God is coming. You used to walk in these ways in life you once lived. But now you must also rid yourselves of all such things as these: anger, rage, malice, slander, and filthy language from your lips. (Colossians 3:5–10)*

In total, there are eleven issues that Paul mentions. Of these eleven issues, he divides them up into two parts—sexual issues and social issues. Paul jumps right into the sexual issues and does not beat around the bush.

Sexual Immorality

He starts off right away by saying, "Put to death whatever belongs to your earthly nature." Want to quiet a crowd? Throw the term *sexual immorality* out there. Why would Paul begin by saying, "Listen, there is something that we need to kill, and it is sexual immorality"? Part of the reason is the generation that Paul lived in. At the time, they had prostitutes at the temples, and sexual immorality was taking place everywhere. We live in a very similar generation—sexual immorality is just as prevalent today. As followers of Jesus Christ, we have been raised with Christ and, therefore, sexual immorality should not be a part of our lives. Paul uses the Greek word *pornea*, which is where we get the term pornography. It includes adultery, homosexuality, and other forms of sexual perversion. What we need to realize is that God created intimacy between a husband and a wife, and God has blessed that intimacy. In the correct context, it is right, and it is beautiful. Outside of the correct context, it leads to destruction.

My dad used to always tell me, "If you play with fire, you will get burned." I remember one time when I was a kid, there was a large portion of our backyard that I was asked to weed. My parents weren't home, and I thought, "If I make a circle around this area of weeds and start a fire, the weeds will be the only things that burn." So, I went out and I got a little gas can, poured some gasoline in a circle around the weeds, lit it, and it started to burn. I did not realize how quickly the fire would ignite and spread.

I didn't realize that I had spilled some of the gasoline on my shoes. I was standing, admiring my work, and telling myself, *Those weeds aren't going to come back for a very long time!* Suddenly, I looked down and noticed my shoe was on fire. It wasn't a blazing inferno, but it went up my leg, and it burned!

I do not look back at that incident and think, "Man, that was a lot of fun, I enjoyed burning my leg." It hurt! This is what Paul is saying—sexual immorality should not be a part of the life of a follower of Christ. You are to put it to death, because it will seriously hurt you.

Stop Eating from Garbage Cans

Paul then moves on a little bit and uses this term called "impurity." Impurity is something that is unclean. Think about the character of God and who He is. God is without sin; God is perfect; God is holy; God is pure. Nothing impure comes out of God, and God is calling His believers to a new way of living. You are a follower of Jesus Christ; therefore, sexual immorality and impurity should not be a part of your life. A believer needs to be characterized by compassion, kindness, humility and gentleness. As believers in Christ, we need to live lives of purity.

For example, in our everyday lives, most of us try to live cleanly. When we eat, we eat off of clean plates. We do not eat off of a garbage can lid. Yet, so many times, figuratively speaking, we eat out of the garbage can itself with our impurity. These should not be a part of a believer's life: sexual immorality, impurity, and lust. The opposite of lust is love. Love gives, and lust takes. God is described as a God of love, and when we lust, we take our focus off of who God is and put it on something else.

Jesus Christ said in Matthew:

"You have heard it said 'do not commit adultery' but I tell you that anyone who looks lustfully has already committed adultery with her in his heart." (Matthew 5:27–28)

Jesus then says if your right eye causes you to sin, gouge it out and throw it away. He is not saying that literally, but it is symbolic of a spiritual eradication of sin. As believers in Jesus Christ, as followers of Christ and because we have been raised with Christ, we are to have newness of life. Our lives should not be characterized as lustful but as lives that show love.

If you look in Scripture, there is so much more that God says yes to than no. For example, in Genesis 3, how many trees did God tell Adam and Eve to avoid? One. Yet, how many trees were there in the garden? We do not actually know, but we do know that while Adam and Eve were in the garden, and while it was a pure and perfect place, they could go to any tree other than that one tree. They could go to any tree and pick from it and eat from it any time that they wanted. God only told them to stay away from one tree. They had access to everything else in the garden. "All of this is yours, except for that one tree."

Satan came along and said, "You will not surely die. For God knows that when you eat of it your eyes will be opened, and you will be like God, knowing good and evil" (Genesis 3:4–5). Their evil desires lead them astray, and they picked fruit from that tree and they ate it.

Kill It—All of It

Next, Paul addresses greed, which is idolatry. Remember the context of this passage: The Colossians were struggling with sexual sins and with greed. Greed is the desire to have more. When you desire to have more, your focus becomes that which you desire to have, which ultimately becomes your god. A. W. Tozer said, "When we strongly desire to own a thing, it actually owns a part of us."

Paul is not giving us any wiggle room here, have you noticed that? He has not said, "I have a great idea, how about we try really hard to stop doing these things?" Paul is saying, "Kill them. Destroy them. Have nothing to do with these things, because they will only tear you down." Many sexual sins are secretive, and we think that no one sees them, but God does. Pastor Bob Johnson often says, "Sexual sin will take you further than you want to go, and cost you more than you want to pay."

Therefore, put them to death, don't just set them aside. Do not bring it out or give it some breath. Kill it and destroy it. Imagine with me that you are holding a vase that represents all those things Paul has talked about: sexual immorality, impurity, lust, evil desires, and greed. A lot of times what we do is hold the vase

> When you desire to have more, your focus becomes that which you desire to have, which ultimately becomes your god.

in our hands and say, "I have got to stop doing this!" We break off a piece and think the problem is solved when, really, all we have done is removed a chunk. We have not put it to death.

Or perhaps we take the vase and think, *I will just break it into three pieces.* When we think of the term *kill*, breaking it into three pieces does not represent the term. The term kill represents taking something and literally destroying it. Finally, we take a hammer and we smash it. We completely destroy the vase. We might think we can get our super glue later and try to put it back together, but it is not going to happen. It is completely destroyed. When Paul makes the statement "put to death," that is what he is referring to. Kill it—all of it.

Get Rid of It

Next, Paul moves on to what we would describe as social issues. In verses 6 through 8 he writes, "Because of these, the wrath of God is coming. You used to walk in these ways, in the life you once lived." You used to. You used to walk in these ways in the life you once lived, "but now you must rid yourselves of all such things as these." Now is not tomorrow, now is immediate. Now you must what? Rid yourselves. Get rid of it. It is a term similar to "put to death." Now you must rid yourselves of not some things but all these things.

My family and I lived in Covington, Kentucky, for about seven years in a house that backed up to a wooded area. After a couple years, we decided to put a nice bird feeder on the back deck. I filled it up every few weeks, and then every few days, and pretty soon it was being emptied every day. I knew that the birds were not eating it at night, so I wondered what was happening. One night at dusk, I looked out at my deck and I saw the problem—*raccoons*. Some of these raccoons would come up and sit at the bottom of the bird feeder waiting for the food to fall. Other raccoons were more creative and would climb up seventeen stairs to the top of my deck and eat straight out of the bird feeder.

I thought, *This is a bird feeder, not a raccoon feeder!* So I went to my neighbor, who was a police officer, and asked his advice. He told me to take antifreeze, put it in a bowl and set it out on the deck. The raccoons would drink it and it would poison them to death. Well, at the time my kids were three and one, and that didn't seem like the best idea. My neighbor then suggested I could just shoot and kill them. So at dusk when they came walking up, one by one, I began shooting, killing, and throwing them into the woods.

Twenty minutes later, another one walked up, using that same path, and I said to him, "Did you not just see your friend killed?" I shot him and threw him deep into the woods, but the raccoons just kept coming and coming and coming. Then I changed my strategy. I decided to lay the next raccoon carcass right in the path. Guess what? I never had raccoon problems again. My goal wasn't to feed them; it wasn't to make them pets. My goal was to get rid of them.

When Paul is talking about these social issues, these everyday issues we all deal with, he says, "But now you must rid yourselves of all such things as these: anger . . ."

This anger Paul describes means seething anger or a person who responds to quick impulses. Many times this anger shows itself with revenge. You may say, "Well, it is the way I grew up." Paul does not say, "But now you must rid yourselves of anger unless, of course, you were raised by an angry person." No. There is no way of getting around it. We are followers of Christ, we have been raised with Christ, and our affections need to be set on things above. We just need to kill that anger.

Next, Paul lists *rage*. Rage and anger are very similar. It is another outburst of passion, but the root word here means "killing." Then he mentions *malice*, the desire to hurt someone intentionally. When we realize we are a part of the body of Jesus Christ and that we are all intricately put together and designed to be a family, why would we want to mistreat other believers, our other brothers and sisters in Christ? If we look at the example of Christ throughout his life, we see that Christ told us to love our enemies and pray for those who persecute us. We do not like that one: unlimited forgiveness. All of these attributes of Christ are all contrary to what Paul is saying to get rid of here.

Then Paul addresses *slander*. Slander is speaking in a way that brings harm to someone else's reputation. My mom would say, "If you do not have anything nice to say, do not say it at all." And, so, guess what I would do? I would not say anything at all, because I was not a believer in Christ. I did not have anything nice to say. Now I am a follower of Christ, and Paul wants me to get rid of those things. Take that slander, get rid of it, and do not let it be a part of your life. Paul goes on and talks about *filthy language, foul speaking,* and *swearing*. Ephesians 4:29 says:

> *Do not let any unwholesome talk come out of your mouths, but only what is helpful for building others up, according to their needs so that it may benefit those who listen.*

The purposes of my mouth and the words that I speak, as commanded in Scripture, are to build people up, not to tear them down. We often say, "I was only joking." Or when we are sarcastic, we might say, "I am just kidding." But there is usually truth in a jest. We need to be careful. When people leave our presence, they should feel encouraged and built up.

Recently I was speaking at Baptist Bible College in Pennsylvania and had occasion to talk to the president of the college. After a short conversation, I walked away realizing he just made me feel as though I was the greatest person in the world. Have you ever been around people like

> The purposes of my mouth and the words that I speak, as commanded in Scripture, are to build people up, not to tear them down.

that? There are some people who just make you feel so good and so encouraged, not to the point of causing you to become egotistical, but in a truly biblical way. That is the way the church should be! Our brothers and sisters in Christ surround us. We build each other up, and if we fall down, crash, and burn, we have people around us who will pick us up, dust us off, and send us on our way to honor Christ. That is the kind of church that we need to be a part of, and we need to continue to breed that environment of building and helping and encouraging.

We Have Put on the New Self

In verses 9 and 10, Paul says:

> *Do not lie to each other, since you have taken off your old self with its practices and have put on the new self, which is being renewed in knowledge in the image of its Creator.*

We all know what lying means, and all of us have been hurt in one way or another by someone lying to us. Paul emphasizes it by telling us not to lie to one another, because we are followers of Christ, and we are in this battle together.

How many of you have made a promise to God to stop some or all of these behaviors, and the next day you did it? "God, I will never swear again, I promise You." Paul says we need to rid ourselves of these things and get rid of them completely. Kill it. It is not a suggestion; it is not a feel good thing. It takes time, and it takes effort. It also takes the body of Christ and immersing ourselves in the Word of God. It takes getting rid of some things and saying no to some things. It might mean getting rid of some friendships or relationships that pull us down. As a follower of Christ, those things Paul lists should not be a part of our lives whatsoever.

It is a battle that I experience every day. But we aren't alone; Paul also battled this. In Romans, Paul said, "I do the things that I shouldn't do, and I do not do the things that I should do" (Romans 7:15–16). It is an everyday battle from the moment that we get up and our feet hit the floor, from the moment that we are driving, going to school, going to work, or going to meetings. There is a battle taking place within the heart of anyone who wants to live out these things. Satan wants us to feed our sexual immorality, impurity, lust, evil desires, and greed. He wants us to be involved in anger, slander, filthy language, lying, and malice. That is what Satan wants for us to do, and Paul tells us, "No! You have a newness of life. When God saved you, you did not get a cosmetic makeover. You got an entire transition, an entire change!" If we claim to be followers of Christ, then we need to put to death these things—otherwise we will continue to struggle for the rest of our lives.

Let us live in such a way that we put all of these things to death and rid ourselves of them so that Jesus Christ may shine as a very bright light in a very, very dark world.

Closing Prayer

Father, all of us struggle in one or more of these areas, and it is a constant battle. There is a battle going on right now for our hearts, but because we have been renewed, and because You desire for us to be conformed into the image of Jesus Christ, I pray that we would put to death these things in our lives that so easily reign over us. May we shine as a bright light in a dark world.

Father, You have saved us to live a life of holiness and righteousness, not to live a life that Paul describes here. If there are some things in our lives that are hindering us from running that race, from moving forward, from honoring and glorifying You, the King of kings and Lord of lords, bring them to our minds and help us to repent of them. Help us to seek counsel from other people and to receive help. Help us to dive into Your Word. We want to look like Your son, Jesus Christ. Thank You for the clarity of Your Word. Now, Lord, we need to live it. We pray in Christ's name, Amen.

October 14, 2007
Cornerstone Baptist Church

Chapter 4

ARE YOU PROPERLY DRESSED?
Colossians 3—Part III

In case you haven't read the first two chapters of Colossians, here is a little recap. This won't cost you a penny! Paul wrote the book of Colossians. In the first two chapters, he sets up the fact that Christ is supreme and He reigns over everything. A lot of mysterious teaching was coming into the church and so Paul tells us all the reasons we know that Christ is supreme.

In Colossians 3 and 4, he tells us: "Now that you understand who the person of Jesus Christ is—live it out!" It's time to huddle. We huddle, huddle, huddle, and then we live it out. A football team never scores any points unless they come out of that huddle and actually do something about it. So Colossians 3 and 4 tell us to put into practice what we've learned. The first four verses deal with setting your heart and your mind on things above. Since you've been raised with Christ, focus your heart and mind on things above. Paul says that's where Christ is seated at the right hand of God.

I have a friend named Kris who has terrible vision. Good vision is 20/20. Kris's vision is 20/400. That's pretty bad. I put his glasses on while preaching the message of this chapter so I could see how they worked for me.

Oh, my goodness! I couldn't recognize anyone in the congregation. I knew my buddy Dave was sitting right there, but I could not tell who anyone was in the room. Now I have pretty good vision. I can read well; I can see stop signs; and I can see stop lights. But with Kris's glasses, you don't want me driving! (And that one Sunday, I had to quickly take his glasses off before I got violently ill.)

The reason that Kris needs to wear his glasses is because there is a problem with his eyes. He puts on the glasses to readjust his eyes so that he can actually see. I probably wouldn't have been able to see the words on the screen. Paul is saying, "Listen folks, you've got to focus on Christ."

Last year, I talked in a message about putting to death certain things. Paul said to put away anger, rage, malice, slander, and filthy language from your lips. He talked about sexual immorality and impurity, evil desires, and greed. We destroyed those things, because if you don't put those things to death—if you don't kill those things—they will kill you. They will reign in your body, and they will ultimately destroy you.

Let's consider some really good news, because this is the "put on" section. This is the clothing section. A question I have for you is: Are you properly dressed? Another question: What are you putting on? Paul makes this statement saying, "Therefore, as God's chosen people, holy and dearly loved, clothe yourselves . . ." Think about that statement, "Therefore as God's chosen people." He calls us chosen people.

> God is always calling His people to look like Him. I'm never to look like anyone else other than Jesus Christ.

It's not a mistake of words. Paul is saying we are God's chosen people. Meaning this: I have been saved by God. My life has been changed by God. I am a follower of Christ. My faith and hope is found in Christ and nothing else. My faith is not in the church, it's not in my senior pastor, it's not in my family, and it's in nothing else other than God. And that's why he calls us God's *chosen* people. That's a huge statement there, because you can only put on certain things if you're a follower of Christ. He also says we are "holy and dearly loved," meaning we are set apart. In 1 Peter 2:10 it says,

Once you were not a people but now you are the people of God; once you had not received mercy, but now you have received mercy.

So Paul is showing contrast: Once you were not a people of God, but now you are a people of God. At one point you did not receive mercy, and at another point you did receive mercy. Paul can say to us: "You were like this before you knew God, but now it's time to get dressed." It's time to *put on*. It's time to clothe ourselves.

There are seven characteristics we learn about in this passage. But these are not exclusive. There are other passages of Scripture that also deal with putting on certain qualities. In the book of Ephesians, we learn about putting on the full armor of God. In Ephesians 6, Paul says if you want to stand, you must be ready for battle. Therefore you need to put on certain things. You need to put on the belt of truth and the breastplate of righteousness; you need to put on the shield of faith, the helmet of salvation, and the sword of the Spirit. You have to put on those things. You have to get ready because there's a battle. The enemy isn't out there shooting little paper wads at you through a straw saying, "Oh, I think I hit him." No, in Ephesians 6, it says he is shooting fiery darts. I don't even really know what that looks like other than maybe in an old movie, but I know fiery darts have got to be bad. They've got to be something that's pretty serious for Paul to say you've got to put these things on.

In Galatians 5, Paul talks about the fruit of the Spirit—love, joy, peace, patience, kindness, goodness, faithfulness, gentleness, and self-control. From the book of Genesis through the book of Revelation, God is showing His people what He wants them to look like. And it's not a matter of how you physically dress. It's not a matter of what church you go to. You know what it is? It's a matter of your heart. God is always calling His people to look like Him. I'm never to look like anyone else other than Jesus Christ.

Put On Compassion

And so it's time for us to get dressed—spiritually speaking. Paul's first statement in our Colossians passage is, "Clothe yourselves with compassion." Now, just think about that word: *Compassion*.

When I read Paul's words leading up to this, I see he is telling us to kill these other things and put our focus on Christ. We are supposed to put these other things to death, but now since we're God's chosen people, holy and dearly loved, we're to clothe ourselves with compassion.

That's great, I guess. But I was hoping more for something like a lion's heart. Clothe yourself with the attitude of a wolverine (shout out to Michigan fans everywhere!). How about putting on something that could really make a lot of noise and do a lot of damage? Why not something everybody will see as it's taking place? But Paul starts with compassion. Why? Well, because God knows this: My heart is already the heart of a wolverine. It's already the heart of a lion. It already wants to fight. It already wants to battle. So he says put on *compassion.*

What is compassion? Compassion is seeing a need and being moved by it. Compassion begins with pity. It begins with feeling sorry for someone. But then it goes beyond that to being moved. Matthew 9:35–38 says,

Jesus went through all the towns and villages, teaching in their synagogues, preaching the good news of the kingdom and healing every disease and sickness.

Think about the lines of people waiting to see Jesus. It says he healed every disease and sickness. You have a sore throat? No problem, just stand in line—He's going to heal you in a little bit. You have a bad knee? He's going to heal it. That would be amazing. He did all these miracles because "when he saw the crowds, He had *compassion* on them." The person of Jesus Christ, God Himself, was moved with pity for these people "because they were harassed and helpless, like sheep without a shepherd."

Christ went into a city and began teaching and healing, and He saw people with needs. He looked at them as though they were harassed and helpless, like sheep without a shepherd. It's really a picture of an animal mauling someone and that person lying in a pool of blood, dying with no hope. And He had compassion on them. But He didn't stop there. He didn't just look with compassion.

This is what He did:

Then he said to his disciples, "The harvest is plentiful but the workers are few. Ask the Lord of the harvest, therefore to send out workers into his harvest field."

Christ was moved with compassion, and what did He do? He did something about it. As we are putting on, as we are clothing ourselves—whether

44

it's the fruit of the Spirit in Ephesians 6 or here in this passage—what are we putting on? What happens when we see a need? What breaks our hearts? Is it our favorite football or baseball team losing? Or is it seeing an unbeliever walking down the street who has no hope?

I have to be honest. There are times when my team loses and my heart breaks. By the way, I'm a Fighting Irish fan. (Thank you to the one person who clapped for me when I mentioned this in my sermon. We'll get a support group together.) Sometimes when they are having a good year, and then they lose a game, it can be heart-breaking. But does my heart break for the things that break the heart of God? I hope it does. As Paul said, "Patrick, you are to clothe yourself." It's not an option; it's not a suggestion. What is it? It's a command.

If there is one occupation where it is important to be dressed properly, I would imagine firefighter would be at the top of the list. Would you agree with me on this? A firefighter would rank high in the area of being completely and properly dressed.

When my son was little, he said to me one time when we were driving along, "Dad, I think I want to be a fireman when I grow up." And I said, "Okay. You know what firemen do?" He didn't really know. I told him they run into burning buildings and help people. He said, "I don't want to be a fireman."

Then he said, "I want to be a policeman." I said, "Do you know what policemen do?" "What?" "They run into burning buildings without the outfits on to rescue people." He decided that day, "I don't want to be a policeman either." Firemen run into buildings to save people. They lay their lives on the line. And if there's a group of people that need to be properly dressed, it's definitely the men and women who run into fires to save lives.

Joe Nothdurft is a good friend who is a fireman. If I offered Joe a pair of flip-flops, I imagine he wouldn't wear them into a fire. Maybe he'd wear my Crocs because they look really good. Probably not. I would imagine that if you go into a fire, you're going to want something that is fire retardant. If I jumped into a fire with a pair of flip-flops on, I probably wouldn't stay very long. If you are going into a fire, you need to have on the proper clothes.

45

Put On Kindness

Paul continues and makes this statement: "Therefore clothe yourselves with compassion and kindness" (Col. 3:12).

Kindness is being courteous—it's being tender. Another way you can really translate this word kindness is "easy." True kindness is a desire to help other people. And being a child of God produces true kindness. Yet you might look at some of these characteristics like compassion and kindness and say, "That's kind of sissy. I don't want to be known as kind; I want to be known as tough! I don't want to be known as compassionate or gentle; I want to be known as a lion."

But Paul is saying, "No. If you're a child of God, if you're a follower of Christ, clothe yourself with kindness."

In Matthew 11:29–30, Christ makes this statement:

"Take my yoke upon you and learn from me, for I am gentle and humble in heart, and you will find rest for your souls. For my yoke is easy and my burden is light."

Christ is saying, "My yoke is easy, it is kind." Now when you see this word *yoke,* what is the first thing that comes to your mind? Eggs! That's what comes to my mind. When I was little and heard someone say that Christ's yoke is easy, I had no idea what that meant. What in the world does that mean to a five-year-old? Even now, what does that mean to a forty-two-year-old? Is He talking about scrambled eggs? Is He talking about egg whites? Or is He talking about egg yolks? What is He talking about?

Picture two huge animals. They look kind of like bulls, but they are called oxen. Now, I grew up in San Jose, California, and to be honest, I never saw oxen except in pictures. But I know enough that if there are two of those huge animals coming down the road, I'm not going to do the whole *running of the bulls* thing that they do in Spain. No, I'm getting out of the way.

However, if these two huge bull-like animals have a wooden bar going across their backs, then that's a whole different deal. That wood is called a *yoke.*

But it's still confusing, because the yoke doesn't look easy, does it? And it doesn't look kind. But this cross-piece goes across both of the animals so they will work together. It allows them to help each other as they're pulling, digging, and tilling the fields. That's what the yoke does. It's a cross-piece that binds the two animals.

Christ is saying, "Take my yoke upon you, because it is kind and it is easy." Only God can say something like that. If I said, "Just take this wood, and it'll be kind and easy. It'll feel good for your shoulders. You can just work and do what you want to do," you wouldn't believe me. Only Jesus Christ can do that.

Paul is telling us to clothe ourselves with kindness. By doing this, it binds you together with others. In 1 Corinthians 13:4, we learn that love is patient and love is kind. It's an attribute that at times we ignore because we'd rather be the opposite of kind. Kindness is not just smiling; it's not just opening the door for someone. Kindness

> Kindness is not just smiling; it's not just opening the door for someone. Kindness is not a weakness. It is an attribute of Jesus Christ.

is not a weakness. It is an attribute of Jesus Christ. All of these attributes, all of these characteristics, point to one person—and it's not you and it's not me. It's ultimately who? Jesus Christ. So if I'm a follower of Christ, then I need to look like Christ. I need to pray, "God, help me to be kind in my dealings with people and the way that I help people."

Have you heard of a Nomex hood? Firefighters wear them. My friend Joe, the fireman, has told me this hood is not just a simple Halloween mask. Rather, it's a hood that goes over your face and over your ears. It provides protection in the middle of a fire. Even NASCAR drivers wear them. If the driver just put on a helmet, he would still be exposed. His cheeks, chin, and throat would all be exposed. So he puts on a Nomex hood to help protect his entire head. But it's not just enough to have on the right boots and the right hood. There is more.

Put On Humility

Paul says, "Clothe yourselves with compassion, kindness, humility." What an incredible attribute, and yet what a difficult thing to model. How do you model humility?

"Hey, everybody—look at me! I'm humble!" That doesn't go over very well. When I was growing up, I had a sign on my door that said, "When you're as great as I am, it's hard to be humble." I saw that every day of my life, and I believed it—that is, until I got to be a little bit older. When I became a follower of Christ, then my desires changed. My ideas changed and my passion changed.

Humility is more than playing golf when you don't know how or trying to ski for the first time. Humility is finding your strength in God and in Him alone. Humble people find their strength in God. Arrogant people find their strength in themselves. And that's a fine line.

I have to be honest—this is something I struggle with every single day of my life. I can be the most arrogant person in the world. I wish I were as humble as the most humble person in the world, Jesus Christ. That is something I need to strive toward.

Genesis 2:7 makes this statement:

The Lord God formed the man from the dust of the ground and breathed into his nostrils the breath of life, and the man became a living being.

So God took what from the ground? Dust. It doesn't say he started with a rock. He didn't find a star from a faraway galaxy. It says He took dust—that which we don't like, that which we want to get rid of—and He formed man. Man wasn't even alive when God formed him out of dust. God basically had to give him CPR. He breathed life into the man, and he became a living being. So when I think that I've got it all together and that I am in charge of the entire universe, I need to realize this: I am dust! God literally created me out of dust! God then had to take His breath and breathe into me to give me life. If you understand this, it will keep you humble, because you realize where you came from.

John Piper was questioned about his own humility, and he made this statement: "I find it difficult to even answer that question. But I will sum it up in one simple sentence. Prayer—pleading with God for humility."

Really? That's the whole deal about humility? That's it? Yes, that is humility. That is what Piper does every single day of his life. Philippians

2:5–8 are great verses that deal with humility in the person of Jesus Christ. Paul says,

> *Your attitude should be the same as that of Christ Jesus: Who being in the very nature God, did not consider equality with God something to be grasped, but made himself nothing taking the very nature of a servant being made in human likeness. And being found in appearance as a man, he humbled himself and became obedient to death—even death on a cross!*

The Son of God, God Himself, left His home, came to this earth, and walked with people like you and me. He experienced the same pain and hunger and thirst that you and I experience. He went to the cross and died for us, and then He rose again. That's what God did for us. So Paul is saying clothe yourselves with compassion, kindness and humility. Clothe yourself with humility, because Jesus Christ is humble. And because it's an attribute that Paul gives us in the book of Colossians, it's a *must*. You have to do it.

Joe would be pretty well equipped with the right boots, Nomex hood, and fire-protective pants. But he needs more than that. He needs a big coat. He wouldn't want to run into the fire with just a tee shirt. The right jacket will protect his shoulders, arms, waist, back, and chest. With this protection, he's almost ready.

Put On Gentleness

Compassion, kindness, humility—but that's not all. We are also to put on gentleness. What? When am I going to put something on that's tough? Sometimes we see gentleness as a weakness, and yet when we are in need, who do we go to for help? We look for gentle people.

I love to have a good nurse around if I'm in the hospital. I haven't been in the hospital in a long time, but when I'm there—I like someone who is kind. I don't want anyone who just got out of running a prisoner of war camp. I don't want a drill sergeant who says, "Get up right now and breathe into this machine." I want someone who is very gentle and kind and who is going to encourage me by saying, "It's going to be alright; it's going to be better."

Paul says we should put on gentleness. In Matthew 5:5, Christ makes a statement: "Blessed are the meek" (or the gentle). This is a fruit of the Spirit, and what's interesting about this fruit of the Spirit is that it never goes out of season. What does a gentle person look like today? Is he a weak person? No. A gentle man is a strong man, because he understands his security is in Christ. I don't need to be strong and courageous, because I realize who my Savior is.

Gentleness is looking out for others' needs. It's helping struggling believers. It's having a teachable spirit. Those are things that we look for in others. In Matthew 21:1–5, Christ is getting ready to go to the cross. He sends His disciples ahead. He tells them to go into Jerusalem to find a donkey and meet a man who understands what's taking place. The passage says,

> *This took place to fulfill what was spoken through the prophet: "Say to the Daughter of Zion, 'See, your king (speaking of Christ) comes to you, gentle and riding on a donkey, on a colt, the foal of a donkey.'"*

Christ will be entering Jerusalem on a donkey. That's kind of different. This is hard for us to understand since we live in metro Detroit. During the times in the Middle East when a king would win a battle, they would come back into town with a type of homecoming parade. The crowds would lay out the red carpet and the branches, play music and the king would enter on a huge horse—sometimes even a white horse. This tradition was to symbolize the battle that was won and to show everyone that the king was the hero. The music would play; people would scream and dance and be all excited. These were probably huge Clydesdale horses. These are beautiful horses, very distinct even from other horses. And definitely much different than a donkey.

A donkey is an animal that needs to be led at times. A horse just runs. A donkey needs to be pulled at times. They are very stubborn. I was a youth pastor in Covington, Kentucky, and every year they would have a big dramatic presentation for Christmas. They used live animals, which is always extremely dangerous, especially for housekeeping. We had goats and pigs, and we even had a donkey.

One time the donkey got loose in the middle of the night. About 2:00 a.m. a guy who had been drinking a little bit too much noticed the donkey and called the police. The officers came, grabbed the donkey, and brought it back to our church. They woke up our director of maintenance and encouraged him to tie up the donkey.

It was Easter, so we had decided that Christ was going to come through the middle of the church riding on a donkey—right through the crowds of people. In fact, there were a couple thousand people in the auditorium. The donkey started walking, and there was a child pulling the donkey. That donkey got about halfway up the aisle and made a decision: *I'm not moving anymore.* This boy pulling the donkey was about twelve years old. That donkey was not going to move. The boy pulled and pulled, but the donkey weighed more than him, plus Jesus was sitting on top of him. He went and got some carrots to tease the donkey, but it still didn't work. So Jesus had to get off the donkey right there and walk the rest of the way into Jerusalem. It kind of changed the story, but that donkey wasn't going anywhere!

Donkeys are stubborn animals! They do what they want. (Of course, if you are Jesus Christ riding the donkey, it will probably move just fine). But a donkey was not a symbol of someone who was going to conquer or be a hero. A donkey was a symbol of humility and gentleness. Christ didn't come into Jerusalem on a big horse. He came gently, riding on a donkey. In this way, Jesus Christ set the example for you and for me.

The donkey was a sign of peace. As the demonstrators stood there when Christ rode in on the donkey, they suddenly realized who He was.

How did Jesus Christ deal with people who might have been a bit aggressive? Remember the story of the Samaritan woman? She had five husbands. One day she was out getting water in the middle of the day when people didn't typically do that. What did Christ do? Did He call her names? Did He abuse her verbally? No, instead He said, "Today I will give

> So many times we are quick to push someone off the cliff—shoot and ask questions later. Instead, we need to be more like Christ.

51

you water, and you'll never thirst again." That's how Christ dealt with the Samaritan woman.

How did Christ deal with the woman who was caught in adultery? The community teachers were gathered around and saying, "What are you going to do with her?" Christ looked at her, and He didn't call her a prostitute or damn her to hell. Instead, He very gently said, "Go and sin no more." That's how Christ dealt with it. So many times we are quick to push someone off the cliff—shoot and ask questions later. Instead, we need to be more like Christ.

Joe is just about dressed. He has the boots, protective pants, Nomex hood, and coat. But he needs a mask. The mask has a voice box, which allows a fireman to talk, breathe, and see clearly. It is a crucial part of the outfit. It doesn't quite complete the outfit, but it is very important.

Put On Patience

There are a lot of things easier than coming to church and realizing God's going to work on you in the areas of compassion, kindness, humility, gentleness, and patience. Whew!! Patience is something I need to work on. Patience is all about restraining yourself. It is responding correctly in a difficult situation. You can tell a lot about someone by how they respond when things get tense.

Let me tell you about the number 696. When we first moved to Michigan, I thought I was a pretty good driver. But let me tell you, I have never been cut off more times in my life than when I'm driving in the Detroit area. I get made fun of, see gestures and words mouthed that I can't repeat, all because I'm not driving fast enough or I inadvertently cut someone off. Just the other day I was on 696 when a car cut in front of me. How do you even fit a car into six inches of space? Detroit drivers always figure out a way to do it. And sometimes I want to honk! But then I remember the horn in my car doesn't work and honking probably wouldn't do any good anyway. Talk about road rage! I need to get my horn fixed. I'll just start honking as soon as I get on 696.

How do you respond in a situation when things are difficult or tense?

What you do or say tells a lot about who you are. God is continuing to shape us and mold us into the image of Jesus Christ. He has called us out of darkness into light. And living a life in the light is living a life of patience. He called us out of being dead to what we are now—alive. He called us from a kingdom of ourselves to His kingdom of people. And so we need to reflect—we need to look, we need to act, and we need to sound—like Jesus Christ. And one of these areas is in the area of patience.

In Mark 6, Christ had been teaching for quite a while. The disciples told Christ to send the people away because He couldn't feed all of them. Christ decided that He was going to feed them. So Jesus fed five thousand people. That was the first church potluck, and wow, what a feast! Can you imagine having five thousand people over for lunch with only a couple of loaves of bread to feed them? You think the communion wafers are small. Can you imagine dividing a couple loaves of bread among all of us here—except with a crowd five times as large? He fed five thousand people. That's significant.

You need to realize that the miracles that Christ did don't happen every day. When was the last time you saw someone who took nothing and created something out of it? When was the last time you saw someone feed five thousand people with just a fish and a piece of bread? When was the last time you saw someone walk on water? You haven't. When we think about these miracles, we need to realize they are significant and only the Son of God is able to do them.

But a short time later in Mark 8, Christ taught again. Jesus had already fed five thousand people. Now, two chapters later, Christ was teaching four thousand people. The disciples saw Christ teaching, and again there was no food. The disciples wanted to get rid of the people, but Christ again wanted to feed them. The crowd was so hungry. The disciples tried to convince Jesus: "Let them get food from some other place. We can't possibly find enough food in this remote place."

What did Christ do? He said, "Sit down. We're going to eat."

You know what He didn't do? He didn't come up to the disciples and rebuke them for not having faith. He didn't make fun of them. He didn't say, "Hello! I just fed five thousand a short time ago. There are only four thousand now. Think I can handle that?"

He didn't do that. Instead, He met their needs. Patience is an area that all of us need to work on, every single day of our lives. We need to reflect and model the person of Jesus Christ. I'm thankful that God is patient with me. Truthfully, I would not be as patient with myself as God is. If I were God, I would probably have gotten rid of Patrick McGoldrick a long, long, long time ago. But He's gracious and patient, and He wants me to be conformed into His image. And one of the characteristics is patience.

Back to our fireman. Joe still isn't quite ready. If he's going to run into a building that is on fire, he needs more than the right boots, pants, coat, mask, and hood. He is also going to need to breathe. If you've ever sat by a campfire, you might have noticed that wind will shift the flames and smoke. You stand on one side thinking you won't get smoke in your face, and a few minutes later you are coughing because of the smoke. Maybe I'm just cursed, but I never can pick the right side of the campfire. I imagine when my friend Joe runs into a fire, he also wants to breathe. Joe has told me he wears an air tank, which gives him access to breathe clean air. Now, with all of this gear, he looks ready. And he almost is.

Put On Forgiveness

Colossians 3 reads, "Bear with each other and forgive whatever grievances you may have against one another. Forgive as the Lord forgave you."

Forgiveness is the heart of the gospel. It is the core of our salvation. God has forgiven us. And forgiven people must always be forgiving people. Let me say that again: *Forgiven* people (if you're a follower of Christ, that's you) must always be *forgiving* people. There's no exception. We aren't told to forgive the little things and hold the big things in. No, it says, "Bear with each other and forgive whatever grievances you may have against one another. Forgive as the Lord forgave you."

We're told to put on forgiveness, yet we tend to hold onto grudges. We want revenge; we want to repay evil for evil. Sometimes our hearts want to get revenge. We want to hold a grudge. And there are times, I know, in my own life when I do *not* want to forgive. There are times in my own life when

I just want to hold on. And you know what happens when I don't forgive? I get angry, and my heart gets bitter. I become an ugly person on the inside, and my heart is just black. Paul is saying bear with each other and forgive whatever grievances you may have with one another.

Ephesians 4:32 says, "Be kind and compassionate to one another, forgiving each other, just as in Christ God forgave you." If our greatest need in this world had been information, God would have sent us an educator. If our greatest need in this world had been technology, God would have sent a scientist. If our greatest need in this world had been money, God would have sent us an economist. If our greatest need in this world had been pleasure, God would have sent us an entertainer. But our greatest need in this world was forgiveness, and God sent us a Savior by the name of Jesus Christ who laid it all out on the cross for you and for me. He laid it all out. So Patrick, why would you not forgive?

Luke 23:34 recounts the time when Christ was attacked and crucified. I don't know that I'll ever really understand how He could say, "Father, forgive them, for they do not know what they are doing."

Father forgive them—those people right down there who are mocking me, who scourged me, who beat me, who punched me, who spit on me, who put me on the cross, and nailed the nails into my wrists and my hands. Forgive them. They don't know what they're doing.

What would you have said? Nuke them. Just get rid of them. We are told Jesus could have sent thousands of angels. He just needed one actually. One angel—*whoosh, whoosh, whoosh*—you're gone. But Jesus doesn't do that. He says, "Father, forgive them, for they don't even understand what they're doing."

Forgiveness is the heart of the gospel. If we are not a forgiving people, we will never be properly clothed for battle as in Ephesians 6 or Colossians 3. What would have been my response? You don't want to know. But Christ's response was "forgive them, for they do not know what they are doing."

Joe has only two more things to put on. His head is still not adequately protected. He needs a helmet. When you go into a house and it's on fire, it's highly likely that the house will start falling apart. Stuff will come crashing down, and it's important that Joe's head is protected. And so as Joe puts on the helmet he's getting close to ready.

Put On Love

Paul ends our passage by saying there is one virtue above all the others. There is one thing to put on that is more important than all the others:

He starts, "And over all these virtues . . ." He is saying the next virtue is above compassion, kindness, humility, gentleness, patience, and forgiveness. It is over all these virtues, over all of them. Over *all* of them—meaning this one is bigger. It's a lot louder; it yells from the mountain top. So get ready.

"Over all these virtues put on love, which binds them all together in perfect unity." It completes it. Love takes the kindness, gentleness, and patience and binds them together in perfect unity. Not just unity. Paul is not just saying they are woven together and it looks good. No, he says this is a perfect unity. Love puts all these other virtues together in perfect unity. Not one thing is missing. As followers of Christ, we are to put on love, because when we put on love, we're clothed and we're ready.

In the passage about the fruits of the Spirit, love is at the very top. In 1 Corinthians 13, it says, "And now three of these remain: faith, hope and love. But the greatest of these is love." Do you think Paul is trying to get a point across? Out of faith, hope, and love, the greatest of these is love. You can clothe yourself with this, that, and the other thing, but love binds them all together, in perfect unity. Love is at the very top.

> If we completely understand and embrace that we are to love God with everything and love our neighbors—it will change everything.

Paul is trying to get a point across to us—it's about love. It's about loving God. In Matthew 22, Jesus is asked, "What's the greatest commandment?" They're trying to trick Him, but He responds, "Love the Lord your God with all your heart, and with all your soul, your mind, and your strength. And the second is like it. Love your neighbor as yourself."

All the law of the prophets hangs on those two commands. Wahoo! So does that mean I can get rid of two-thirds of the Old Testament? No—not at all. But all the Law, everything that was put there, all the law of the prophets, hangs on those two commands.

If we completely understand and embrace that we are to love God with everything and love our neighbors—it will change everything. We will radically change our world like we've never seen before. So what holds me back? It's my stupidity and my own selfish desires.

In John 10:11, Jesus is talking about the relationship between the sheep and the shepherd. He makes this statement: "I am the good shepherd. The good shepherd lays down his life for the sheep."

What does that mean? It is ultimate sacrifice. It is the good shepherd, Jesus Christ, laying His life down for the sheep. There's a contrast in the next verse, where it offers an analogy: If a hired hand watches the sheep and somebody comes along to steal them, what does the hired hand do? He says, "I'm out of here! I don't get paid enough to watch these sheep, so I'm gone."

But what does Christ do? He protects His sheep. He helps the sheep. Sheep are somewhat dumb animals. You know what you and I are? We're sheep. And the Good Shepherd gave His life. The ultimate sacrifice is love, and that's what Christ did for us. He paid the price for us on the cross—that's what Christ did.

What Are You Putting On?

Let me ask you a question. What are you putting on? Are you properly dressed? Are you putting on compassion, kindness, humility, gentleness, patience, and forgiveness? Are you putting on love that binds all these characteristics together in perfect unity? If not, then you're not completely dressed.

The final thing our fireman needs is gloves. When Joe runs into a fire, he might have to hold a hose or an axe. It's possible he might need to move some hot debris in order to save a life. Even with the right boots, pants, coat, and helmet—he wouldn't be much good without the right gloves. Now, Joe is completely ready to fight a fire. He's fully equipped. He's dressed and ready for battle.

As followers of Jesus Christ, our desire and passion is to be ready, to be willing to do whatever He asks of us. Joe is ready for battle. Are you?

Closing Prayer

Father, we have seen a modern day picture of what a fireman looks like and what he has to do to be ready to go into a fire. We would never jump into a situation like a fire without being completely prepared. And yet, Lord, even in my own heart, there are many times that I try to go into battle and I'm not properly dressed. My mind is not ready. I pray we would realize that compassion, kindness, humility, gentleness, patience, forgiveness, and love are the true picture of your Son, Jesus Christ. Father, it would be our desire to reflect that. We pray in Christ's name, Amen.

August 17, 2008
Cornerstone Baptist Church

Chapter 5

THE GREATEST THING
IS TO KEEP THE GREATEST THING
THE GREATEST THING
Matthew 22

A couple of weeks before my wife and I were married, a woman walked up to me and asked, "Do you have enough staples in your apartment?" Now Dena was living in Chicago, I was living in Pennsylvania, and the wedding was in Iowa. I had been thinking if we could get married on another continent, it probably would have been easier, and this woman asks, "Do you have enough staples in your apartment?"

I was twenty-three, and a lot was going through my mind at that point. First thing was "staples." Staples . . . stapler . . . Swingline stapler. And I thought, *Who cares? Who cares if I have staples in my apartment?*

I had a couch, a bed, a television. I had a refrigerator, even a washer and dryer. There was a shower and a toilet and all those things. I had the necessary things. Okay, I really didn't know what she meant. When you don't know what somebody means, you ask a follow-up question. So I asked, "Could you be more specific?"

Right then, she had this look. She realized that I didn't get it. "Do you have the necessary items like flour, bread, toilet paper, sugar, peanut butter, jelly, Krispy Kreme . . . you know, good stuff like that." I said, "Yes, I do. I have all the necessary staples that I need to basically survive."

Some passages of Scripture have been staples in my life. When I am talking to someone and the person needs a little bit of direction or asks,

"What is something I can read?" I always go to certain passages. They are the staple passages of my life.

The first is Genesis 1, the creation of man. Genesis 3 records the fall of man. Psalm 1 is a description of the blessed man. In Isaiah 6, Christ is seated on the throne, and the angels are flying around Him saying, "Holy, Holy, Holy is the Lord Almighty. The whole earth is full of His glory."

In John 10, Christ describes Himself as the Good Shepherd. In John 14, Christ declares, "I am the way, the truth and the life." In Colossians 3, we're instructed to set our hearts and our minds on heavenly things. In Matthew 4, the temptations of Jesus Christ are described.

The staple passage I want to focus on now is Matthew 22, where Jesus Christ was being questioned about the greatest commandment.

The lesson from this staple passage is this: *The greatest thing is to keep the greatest thing the greatest thing.* Often, we take the lesser things in life and make them the greatest thing. And when the greatest thing is not ultimately the greatest thing, it's not the greatest thing. It's so easy to make those things that aren't the greatest the greatest—things like your hobbies, your family, your friends, relationships, the latest cell phone, the latest video game, or academics. Now some of those are important, but are they the greatest? No.

Matthew 22 records the beginning of the last week of the life of Jesus Christ. He was delivering some of His final public teaching. Christ was talking about taxes and resurrection, and the Pharisees, the Sadducees, the Herodians, and the scribes were listening. All the big dogs from all the religious groups had come together, and usually the only reason they would ever come together was to debate.

Matthew reports that the crowds were amazed at His teaching. It's as though their jaws dropped not only to the floor but fell even to the middle of the earth. However, the religious leaders are not so blown away. Their ultimate desire was to kill Christ.

Now let me ask some questions: Christ raised people from the dead. Have you ever done that? Wouldn't you be happy if it was your relative He brought back to life? I would think that would be a great thing. I would think they would throw a party for Him.

Did Christ heal all diseases and sicknesses? Is that a good thing? We don't need any doctors, dentist, chiropractors, or herbal life specialists. Jesus can heal. Is that a good thing? You better believe it. He even cast out demons. Is that a good thing? You better believe it.

So Christ did all those good things, and what did all those religious leaders want to do? Kill Him. I want to say, "HELLO? Do you understand all the good that He is doing?"

The Greatest Law

Matthew 22:34 records that Jesus had silenced the Sadducees. I love that. You get a bunch of religious talkers around, and all of a sudden they are mum. Actually, it is a picture as though He muzzled them. When a dog gets out of control in the vet's office, you put a muzzle on the dog so it can't open its mouth to bite you.

Then Matthew says the Pharisees gathered. That couldn't be good. So one of the Pharisees, an expert in the law, tested Him with this question, "Teacher, which is the greatest commandment in the law?" They didn't send a first-year law student. They didn't say, "Okay, we are going to draw straws, and whoever has the shortest straw has to go up to this person. You need to have a really good question." They didn't ask for volunteers. What did they do? They got an expert in the Law—and not *just* an expert lawyer, but an expert lawyer who was trained in the Law, in the Old Testament Scriptures. So they were saying, "We want the best person to represent us."

The Pharisees probably had to be excited because the Sadducees were silent. They had argued with God, and when you argue with God, you always lose. So it was their turn, and the Pharisees tested Him with a

> When you argue with God, you always lose.

question. Really when it says they tested Him, it means they tried to trick Him. They wanted to see His jaw drop because they had stumped Him.

"Teacher, which is the greatest commandment in the law?" The Jewish people had 613 laws—248 were positive, and 365 were negative. I went on the Internet, and I searched for "613 laws." On the first Web site, all the laws appeared, so I decided I was going to read them. It was interesting, then it was boring, and then it got kind of funny.

Here are a couple of examples. You are not allowed to eat a worm found in fruit. Oh, I was really hoping to get a little more protein out of that apple. You are not to swear needlessly. So you can swear purposely? You are to examine a witness thoroughly. "Are you innocent?" "Yes." "Are you guilty?" "No." That probably wouldn't go over. Now here's my favorite one. You are not allowed to eat winged insects.

They had laws about signs, symbols, family, seasons, diet, and speech. Of all the 613 possible laws to question Christ about, they instead asked, "Which is the greatest one?" Was it to keep the Sabbath? Or was it the command that brought the greatest punishment if you broke it? "If you do this, you will die." Whatever it was, the Pharisees wanted to know which command was the greatest.

What did Christ do? He didn't gather the disciples. He didn't say, "Give me a moment." He went back to Deuteronomy 6:5. "Love the Lord your God with all your heart and with all your soul and with all your mind and with all your strength." Christ didn't give them a new answer. He answered their question with the Word of God.

That's what I love about Matthew 4. When Christ was tempted, He didn't say, "Get away from me, Satan." He went back to the Word of God, just like He did when He was asked about the greatest commandment. This passage in Deuteronomy 6 is precious to the Jewish people. It is known as the *Shema*. Every morning and every evening, they would quote it. So they knew it in their heads, they spoke it with their lips, but its meaning was far from them. Loving God is the greatest thing. No matter what you get done in a minute, in an hour, in a day, in a week, in a month, in a year, if it's not loving God, then guess what? It's not the greatest. That's why it's one of my staple passages.

God Is Worthy of Our Love

Why is loving God the greatest command? I think one reason it's the greatest command is because God is worthy. And because He is most worthy, He is most worthy of our love. I can love certain things, I can love my family and I can love my hobbies. I can love all of these things and those are okay.

In the Scriptures, throughout the Old Testament, the psalmist in different passages asks, "Who is like you, O God?" and the answer to that is "no one."

Let's look at some of the passages in Scripture that ask this question: "Who is like you, O God?" And the answer is going to be "no one."

Exodus 15:11 declares God is most worthy: "Who among the gods is like you, O Lord? Who is like you—majestic in holiness, awesome in glory, working wonders?" Who is like You? And the answer is "no one."

Psalm 35:10 says, "My whole being will explain . . ." (My whole being . . . WOW, that's big.) "My whole being will explain, who is like you, Lord? You rescue the poor from those too strong and from those who rob them." Who is like You? And the answer is "no one."

Psalm 71:19 says, "Your righteousness, God, reaches to the heavens, you who have done great things. Who is like you, O God?" And the answer again is "no one."

Psalm 89:8, says, "Who is like you, O Lord God almighty? You, Lord, are mighty and your faithfulness surrounds you."

So when you ask, "Why should I love God?" the answer is because He is most worthy. He is most worthy of my praise. He is most worthy of my honor. He is most worthy of my love. We see the awesomeness of God in these verses. And we see that there is no one like Him.

God Loves Us

Why is loving God the greatest commandment? It's because He is most worthy. Another reason is that loving God brings us the most benefit. "Isn't that a bit selfish?" No, it's not. In 1 John 4:19, we read, "We love because God first loved us." God set His love on us, and His eye has never wandered from us. When we lie down and when we sit, when we walk and when we sleep, the eyes of God are constantly upon us. When we drive and when we work, when we are emailing and when we are texting, the eyes of God are constantly, constantly upon us.

Followers of Christ don't always feel that God loves them. One reason is the lack of understanding of God. If you want to understand Him and you want to understand His love, then you've got to get into the Book that describes Him. The other reason we don't always feel God's love is sin. There are times when I question whether God really cares about me. And it's during those times when my life is not a reflection of His glory; I'm not loving Him with all my heart. Sin always tries to quench my love for God and make me question His love for me. If we are living with unconfessed sin, our love for Him is always going to be affected. There are those who know the facts about God, they know the verses and they know the theology. They've dotted the *i*'s, they've crossed all the *t*'s, but guess what? There is no delight in God because they really don't know Him. That describes the Pharisees, the Sadducees, the Herodians, and the scribes. They knew it, they could speak it, they could talk about it, they could argue with it. But when it came down to it in their hearts, they were very far from knowing Him.

And then there are those who truly want to delight in God, who want to feel God, who want to experience God. They want to come away saying, "WOW, that was incredible!" But they don't know Him either. There is no foundation. When I come into church, when I am praying or when I am reading the Word, do I want to experience God in an incredible way? You'd better believe it. Do I want to walk out of here with my mind being stimulated, my thought process thinking through critical issues? You'd better believe it. So there's a balance between what we call spirit and truth.

How Do I Love God?

Another question I have is this: How do I love God? If you were to ask people on the street, friends in your workplace, "How do you love God?" I guarantee you they would come up with some pretty interesting ideas. But Christ gave the answer in Matthew 22:37: "Love the Lord your God with all your heart and with all your soul and with all your mind." Christ is talking about the heart. The heart is the core of your being. It is the base of who you are. Proverbs 4:23 says, "Guard your heart for it is the wellspring of life." We are to guard it because of the importance of the heart. Things you put in, things you allow yourself to see, things you allow yourself to listen to—guard that heart, because it is the wellspring of life.

Bill Bright, who founded Campus Crusade for Christ, wrote about the heart in a little pamphlet. He said we should think about our hearts as thrones. Who reigns on that throne? Do you reign, or does Christ reign? And we sometimes mix that up. I say to myself, "I want to reign!" I won't come right out and say that in my mind, but in my heart, that's sometimes how I feel. Who is reigning in my heart? I am.

I have always enjoyed this preacher who tells you every once in a while you've got to wave that white flag. Because you know what? If you don't wave that white flag and surrender to God, you'll always lose the battle. Love God with all of your heart. God wants to be loved from that place where Christ rules. He doesn't want a second-hand love. Christ needs to be the ruler in our hearts.

Then He says we are to love God with our entire soul. The soul is your emotions. In Matthew 25, Christ was in the garden about to be arrested, and in His prayer, He said His soul was grieved to the point of death. In Psalm 103:1, David cried out, "Bless the Lord, O my soul, and all that is within me, bless His holy name." David was trying to fire up his worship. *Hey soul, O my soul, bless the Lord.* Soul—my emotions, my passion, those kinds of things—soul, I want to bless the Lord. And he said it again in verse 2 just in case we didn't notice it. I wonder why he would say it twice. Do you think repetition is the key to learning? Definitely!

> God wants to be loved from that place where Christ rules. He doesn't want a second-hand love.

The angels in Isaiah 6 said, "Holy, holy, holy is the Lord God almighty." They said "holy" three times. During that period, people would repeat themselves for emphasis rather than raise their voices. As I was growing up, my mother, instead of yelling at me, would say, "You are a bad boy." If I had done something a little worse, she would say, "You are a bad, bad boy." And then, "You are a bad, bad, bad boy." It meant I was in deep weeds, in deep trouble, and no one was going to rescue me.

In Psalm 103, David repeated himself: "Bless the Lord, O my soul, and all that is within me, bless His holy name." David was crying out with his soul, the seat of his emotions. David simply didn't just want to understand the things of God and know the things of God; David wanted to be passionate for the things of God.

I don't want to stand here and just sing because it's the right thing to do. I want my soul to bless the Lord. I want the bottom of my emotions to bless the Lord. That was David. He was a shepherd. Then he was a king, and then he was on the run after he committed adultery and murder. He said, "God, I just want to bless You because of who You are. I want to say it with passion." And that's what Christ was referring to when He was answering the Pharisees, that passion that we have.

I'll be honest, there are times in my life when I am not saddened over my sin. There are times when I enjoy sin. Sometimes, I am sure everyone is more in tune with the things of the Lord than I am. I am just telling you what's in my heart, and there are times when I want to sin. It's when I am not loving God with all my heart and with all my soul. If we never have feelings for God, tears of joy over His goodness, the passion for His will, the light in His Word, sadness over sin—if those things don't move us, then are we really loving God with our soul, with our emotions, with our passion?

"Love the Lord your God with all your heart and with all your soul and with all your *mind*." This is your intellect. It's not checking out. It's engaging your mind in spiritual things. One way to do that is to read solid Christian books, books that will challenge your thinking, introduce you into some of the principles of the Word of God, and tell you how to apply them to your finances, your time management, and other areas of your life. Those books are available so that I can take my mind and love God more with my mind, as I understand the things of God more and more and more. And so the question is, "What do we fill our minds with?" In Colossians 3, Paul said, "Set your minds on things above, not on earthly things." There is a huge contrast between things above and things below.

Maybe you've heard this said before: "Faith is for people who don't think." Some people actually believe that. I think just the opposite is true. Because of my faith, I want to think; I want to fill my mind with the things that are right.

Content with 99 Percent

"Love the Lord your God with all your heart and with all your soul and with all your mind." Notice the word "all." With how much of your heart? With how much of your mind? With how much of your soul? A little bit? How about 99 percent? But 99 percent is not a perfect grade. The perfect grade is 100 percent.

Christ was asking them, "You want to know what the greatest commandment is? Here it is: Are you ready? Love God with all your heart (not a portion of it) and with all of your soul (not a portion of it) and with all of your mind, every part of it." In other words, 100 percent.

A lot of times we are content with 99 percent. Partial obedience is always disobedience. So Christ was saying, "Love Me with all abandonment." When I hear that, does that mean that the only thing I do is just walk around and sing songs to the Lord? How am I loving God with everything? It doesn't mean that every moment of the day all I focus on is the Lord. You can't do that.

You're a math teacher. You are working through a problem, and maybe it's a problem for you, and you are really trying to think through this a little bit. Can you honestly say that during that time, you are completely 100 percent focused on God? God is not asking that we walk around, build a fire, sit around singing "Kumbaya." What it means is that when I am focused on God—whether it's here at church, or it's reading His Word, or I am studying, or having conversation with people—I am giving all that I can to Him. Don't allow distractions during your time of worship or during your time of prayer.

I get fired up about a lot of things in life. I get fired up about my golf swing. The older I get with life and family, the less time I have to play. But when I get out there, I enjoy it. And when the guy I am playing with hits a great shot, and he's like "Beat that, Patrick," and I follow up with a better shot, I just want to say, "IN YOUR FACE! I BEAT YOU!" I don't say it, but I do get fired up about golf.

I get fired up about Notre Dame football. Sorry. (Hey, Michigan fans, you are commanded to love me because we just read that Scripture, so be careful what you think or what you say.) I get fired up about my family. I get fired up about soccer. I get fired up about work. I get fired up about all of those things. Are those okay? Yes they're all right.

But my greatest passion, my greatest effort when we think about "all your heart, all your soul, all your mind," needs to go into loving God. What I am most passionate about can't be my golf swing, or my favorite team, or my kids or my wife or my family. It needs to be the Lord.

I want to be described as a man who loves God. Each of God's people should be described as a man or a woman who loves God, because the greatest thing is to keep the greatest thing the greatest thing. Don't get sidetracked. Don't go off on the shoulder of the road. It's no fun, there's danger over there. Don't veer to the left or veer to the right. When the greatest thing becomes something else and we get sidetracked, we are not doing the greatest thing. And we are not expressing to God His worth, and it's not benefitting us, and we are not loving Him with everything we can.

> I want to be described as a man who loves God.

The Second Greatest Commandment

Christ wasn't content simply to answer their question. He pointed them not only to the greatest commandment but to the second greatest one as well. If I had been the Pharisees or the Sadducees or the Herodians or the scribes, I couldn't take anything else at that point. But Christ pointed them to the second commandment, which He said is just like the first: "Love your neighbor as yourself." "Love the Lord your God with all your heart and with all your soul and with all your mind" and "The second is like it." It is not second as in importance. It doesn't mean that this is first and that is second place. "What place did you come in?" "Second place." "How many teams were there?" "Two." "Congratulations." But no, it's not about importance.

"Love your neighbor as yourself." Last week, my daughter, Paige, and I drove over to work out at this place near our house. As I pulled up, I noticed lots of cars outside the gym even though it is a small place with probably only twenty treadmills. As we walked in, all the treadmills were filled, and I said, "New Year's resolutions."

I ran into this girl who used to go to our church, and I said, "New Year's resolutions?" And she said, "Yep." She said she and her friends all have bets for how long it will last, and she told me if we returned in two weeks, probably nobody would be there.

Do you know why so many people were there? They care about themselves. They decided they were going to make a New Year's resolution. "I am going to work out eight days a week, twenty-five hours a day." "I am going to get back to that high school weight." You are seventy-four years old, so that's probably not going to happen. I've got to be honest with you. Things have happened. Things have changed. Life is different. Struggles take place. But we care about ourselves. We do things to better ourselves, to improve ourselves. We do it, and you want to know why? Because we love ourselves. I'll stand right here, and I will be the first to say, "I love myself." I take care of myself. I want to better myself. Do you understand what I am saying?

So Christ tells us what the greatest commandment is: "Love the Lord your God with all your heart and with all your soul and with all your mind," and the second is, "Love your neighbor as yourself." Do you ever read these passages of Scripture and ask, "Are you kidding me? Are you serious? This is hard to do." Here's the test: If you truly love God, do you love others?

"Others" refers to everyone. Do you love your wife the way you love yourself? Do you love your husband the way you love yourself? Do you love your mom the way you love yourself? Do you love your dad the way you love yourself? What about your brother? What about your sister? What about your in-laws? What about your outlaws? What about all of them? What about that neighbor on your street? I think everyone of us has one of *those* *neighbors*. I have one. Just one. It's difficult.

But loving *that* neighbor or whoever is the difficult person in your life is not an option. And the litmus test is basically this: "Do you say you love God?" "Yes." "Then you will love your neighbor as yourself." If we love God but we don't love others, guess what we are? Liars. So if I say I love God with all my heart and with all my soul and with all my mind—all abandonment, pure abandonment—but I don't love others, I am a big fat liar. I am not telling the truth.

And believers, followers of Christ, are to be known for their love and for their care and for their concern. If you look in the Scriptures, you see we are commanded to love and care for the poor and the needy and the widows. It's not a suggestion; it's a command.

In Matthew 22:40, Christ said that "all the law and the prophets hang on these two commands." That powerful statement was basically Christ's way of saying to the religious leaders, "You have 613 laws, and I have just reduced them to two." Those other laws that are found in Scripture are definitely important. The Ten Commandments are extremely important. Then He said all the law and all the prophets—all the law that they knew and all the law that had been written, all the law of God and of the prophets—all of that hangs on these two commands: Love God and love your neighbor.

Matthew's account ends there, but Mark finished the story in chapter 12 and tells us from then on, no one dared to ask Him any more questions. The big dog stepped forward—the greatest lawyer the religious leaders had—and they were certain he could trick Jesus. "What's the greatest commandment?" "Love God with all your heart and with all your soul and with all your mind. Love your neighbor as yourself."

I like it when those who are wrong lose. I like it when the villain at the end of the movie dies or when the bad guy is obliterated. I like that because that's how it's supposed to end. But the focus isn't that. The focus is Christ. And when questioned and put into a corner, He comes out by quoting Scripture.

> If you want to know how to understand and how to love God more, you need to know Him more.

So what do I do to love God more? How can I get started loving God? Let me tell you the greatest thing that you can do. The Word of God is the secret. If you want to know how to understand and how to love God more, you need to know Him more. If you want to love and understand God and want to have more passion for the Lord, then you need to understand what He has left us in His Word. This is not a list of do's and don'ts. This is a love letter from God to us as followers of Jesus Christ. It is written to us.

Husbands, what if after you said "I do" on your wedding day, kissed your bride, and went off on your honeymoon, you came back and said, "I love you, but I am not going to talk to you for the rest of my life"? How would that go over? And how well would you know that person? And how well would you love that person? You wouldn't.

How Do We Love Others?

As followers of Christ, we need to dive into the Word and pray so that we are communicating with God and growing in our love for Him daily. I would encourage you also to memorize Scripture, some of those staple passages I mentioned earlier. Matthew 22 would be a perfect place to start if you want a passage to understand, to memorize, to know, to hide in your heart, to dig into and to chew on and think about. Just memorize it. You want to love other people? Do an act of service. Just go out of your way and *help* somebody. You know a lot of the answers, and I know a lot of the answers. But often times I don't do it.

Take a small piece of paper and on it write, "Love God." Take it and put it someplace where you will see it often. Maybe it needs to be in your wallet next to your credit card. Maybe it needs to be on the dashboard of your car. Maybe it should be on your mirror where you will see it before you start your morning. Maybe you should put it someplace at work.

When questioned about the Scriptures, Christ quoted from Deuteronomy 6:

> *Love the Lord your God with all your heart and with all your soul and with all your strength. These commandments that I give you today are to be on your hearts. Impress them on your children. Talk about them when you sit at home and when you walk along the road, when you lie down and when you get up. Tie them as symbols on your hands and bind them on your foreheads. Write them on the doorframes of your houses and on your gates. (Deut. 6:5–9)*

Do you think God wants to get the point across that He wants to be loved? When you sit down, when you get up. When you walk, when you run, when you are lying down. During all of those times, loving God is to be the focus of our attention.

I have an idea: We could just take these "Love God" papers and lick them a little bit and stick them right on our foreheads. Or better yet, get a stapler and staple them right on our faces. I'm guessing that won't go over very well. It would look a bit weird and might interfere when we go to work.

But that is the idea. We are commanded to bind them on our foreheads, put them on the doorframes, meaning this: God wants us to see His Word everywhere. You think God wants to get a point across? When Jesus was questioned by those religious leaders in their effort to trick Him, He took 613 laws and explained it all comes down to just 2 laws: Love God and love your neighbor.

We have a command to obey, and that command is to love God. Let's love Him with all of our hearts, all of our souls, and with all of our minds. And let's love our neighbors as ourselves.

In other words, *the greatest thing is to keep the greatest thing the greatest thing!*

January 11, 2009
Cornerstone Baptist Church

Chapter 6

A MARRIAGE THAT HONORS GOD
Four Questions Every Couple Should Be Asking

It was a cold, January morning in Michigan. The sun was not shining. I was sitting in my office when the phone rang. It was my pastor, Bob Johnson. I picked up the phone, and he said, "Patrick, I have a question for you: Would you preach for me?" Immediately I answered, "Yes!" because I enjoy preaching in the main church service. It is a good opportunity for me to grow, be challenged, and preach to a much bigger group than high school or middle school students. Then he said, "It is during the family series. I need you to preach on the topic of the husband/wife relationship and the image of Jesus Christ."

The first thing that took place when I heard that title was instant conviction. Why? Because I realize that every day, I fail. As a husband, I fail. As a father, I fail. As a believer, I fail. As a child of God who is supposed to proclaim the glory of His name, I fail. And yet, I realize that part of the Christian life *is* failing; part of the Christian life is growing day by day. When I hung up the phone, I sat there thinking, *I can't believe he did this. I can't believe Bob asked me to preach this message.* But then I decided, *For the next month and half, I'm going to have a good marriage, because I'm really going to strive to do the right thing.*

It Does Not Matter Who You Are

Have you noticed there are a lot of different people in the world and a whole variety of marriage relationships? There is the couple that holds hands constantly and is excited to be together. They say "I love you" while winking and blowing kisses. They genuinely want a phenomenal marriage. They both want to give 100 percent. Theirs is not a "give and take" relationship but rather "give and give."

Then there is the couple where one spouse gives 100 percent, but the other person only gives 50 percent. There is another couple where one gives 50 percent and their spouse gives a mere 5 percent and lives with a view that marriage can be accomplished with a few minutes of interaction a day.

There are some of you who are alone. Maybe it is because of divorce. Maybe it is because your spouse does not involve themselves in church. Some of you are alone and unmarried because you are too young to be married. Maybe you are single. Maybe you are widowed. If you are currently alone, for whatever reason, remember you were created in the image of God. You are fearfully and wonderfully made, and you are alone because God has designed it that way for you right now. You may wonder how this message applies to you, and, to be truthful, there are some specifics that will not apply to you. At the same time, there are many truths and principles that will definitely apply to you.

No matter who you are, God's Word is clear: If we want our marriages to reflect Christ and the church, then we need to love our spouses just as Christ loved the church.

Marriage God's Way

There is a popular children's toy that has been on the market for a long time—the Tupperware Shape-O-Ball. Basically, the Shape-O-Ball is a hollow ball with shapes cut out of it, and it comes with separate shapes corresponding to the cut-outs. When you look at the Shape-O-Ball, it seems simple. The oval is supposed to go in the oval, and the star is supposed to go in the star, and the square is supposed to go in the square, and the circle is supposed to go in the circle, and so on. As children, it takes time to learn that the oval does not go into the star slot and the square does not fit in the oval slot.

A lot of times, we try to approach marriage like the young child trying to put the wrong shape into the wrong slot—we try to do marriage our way, instead of God's. That is not the way that God has designed marriage. *God has created marriage, and marriage is good.* John Piper said something like this: "Marriage is like a metaphor or a picture that stands for something more than a man or a woman becoming one flesh. It stands for the relationship between Christ and the church." That is the deepest meaning of marriage. It is meant to be a living drama of how Christ and the church relate to each other. Marriage isn't simply just getting married and becoming one flesh, it is a picture and demonstration of Jesus Christ and the church.

> Marriage isn't simply just getting married and becoming one flesh, it is a picture and demonstration of Jesus Christ and the church.

Do You Want a Biblical Marriage?

Is your marriage like that? The overall question I have for us today is this: "Do you want a biblical marriage?" You may say, "Patrick, if you saw my marriage, if you saw the battle that I have every day when I go home, you wouldn't ask this question. Yes, I want a biblical marriage, but I can't do it anymore." Husbands say this of their wives, and wives about their husbands. Men, you need do your part to love your wives as Christ loved the church. Ladies, you also need to do your part to lovingly submit to your husbands as the church does to Christ. When that happens, marriage fits together the way God has designed it; the way that God has established it.

Four Questions

Now, there are four questions that I want you to consider. Spend some time in the Word with them. Go over the questions with your spouse. For those of you in middle school, just keep these for down the road when you get married—hopefully not too soon!

Is Your Spouse Number One in Your Life?

Matthew 19:3–6 says, "Some Pharisees came to him to test him. They asked, 'Is it lawful for a man to divorce his wife for any and every reason?'" What an interesting question. The Pharisees came to "trick" Jesus Christ.

They hated Him. It was a venom-kind of hatred. They despised Him. Their question was, "Is it lawful for a man to divorce his wife for any and every reason?" Think about "any" and "every" reason. Someone today might ask, "My husband didn't pull the car in the way I wanted it to be pulled in. Can I divorce him?" Or, "My wife didn't put the toothpaste on the *right* side of the sink. Can I divorce her for that?" This is what the Pharisees were saying: Can a man divorce his wife for any and every reason?

Look at the response of Christ:

"Haven't you read," he replied, "that at the beginning the Creator 'made them male and female,' and said, 'For this reason a man will leave his father and mother and be united to his wife, and the two will become one flesh'? So they are no longer two, but one. Therefore what God has joined together, let man not separate."

I love the response of Jesus: "Haven't you read?" Who was He talking to? He was talking to the Pharisees. They were the religious leaders. Christ was saying, "Duh! Think about it. Haven't you read this already? You are supposed to know this. You are the teachers of the law. This is what you are all about, and you should be teaching this truth to the people."

Christ then made the statement, "At the beginning the Creator made them male and female? For this reason a man will leave his father and mother and be united to his wife, and the two will become one flesh." That is kind of interesting, because when God created male and female, he created Adam and Eve. He was their heavenly Father. They didn't have a physical mother and father. So how could they leave their mothers and fathers and be united to each other? Well, that verse wasn't specifically for them, it was for us! What Jesus was saying was, "Live in such a way that there is no other human relationship in any way that compares in importance to your husband or to your wife."

> Husbands and wives are not to have two purposes; they are not to have two life directions, going in the opposite direction.

Now, it does not mean that you have to move across the country once you get married. It does not mean that you do not call your parents. It does not mean that you do not send cards. Be a part of your parents' lives. What it *is* saying is that your relationship with your parents, children, or friends should not even *come close* to your relationship with your husband or wife. The way I love my wife should be totally different than the way I love my mother or father or the way I treat my kids. Is your spouse number one in your life?

Christ did not end there. He continued, "For this reason a man will leave his father and mother and be united to his wife." This is cementing. What God brings together is good, and what God establishes is good, and what God creates is good. And it is perfect.

Jesus went on in verse 6, saying, "They are no longer two, but one. Therefore, what God has joined together let not man separate." Husbands and wives are not to have two purposes; they are not to have two life directions, going in the opposite direction. They are not to have two independent dreams; they are to be one in every way. And who puts them together? God does. Let me ask you a question: Who wants to mess with what God has cemented together forever? I don't. I don't want to touch that with a thousand-foot pole. So as we are asking the question "Do you want a biblical marriage?"—men, you do your part to love God with all your heart, soul, mind and strength; to love your neighbor as yourself; to love your wife, to care for her, to take care of her, to meet her needs. Wives, do the same.

Is your husband or wife number one?

Consider this example of a married couple, Jim and Jan:

Jim: *I work all day, and all I ask is for a hot meal to be on the table when I get home.*

Jan: *Here you go. Here's your dinner, honey. I hope you enjoy.*

Jim: *What is this stuff? Are you trying to kill me with this?*

Jan: *Oh, don't be silly, of course I'm not. I had to improvise a little because the fridge has been broken for about three weeks now.*

Jim: *Oh, please. Nag, nag, nag, nag, nag, nag. That's all you ever do these days. Do you think I have nothing else to do?*

Jan: No, I know you have other things to do, and I really appreciate all you do around the house. It is just that I was really hoping to get the fridge fixed. Maybe I could call somebody and have them come out and fix it for us.

Jim: Hey, there is no way we are going to call somebody to fix that fridge when I am perfectly capable of doing it myself.

Jan: Well, you know, some things are worth the money.

Jim: You know, the way you spend my money is incredible. Like what happened last night.

Jan: Well, I think taking our son to the ER was probably a pretty good investment.

Jim: I'm telling you, in my day, we worked through the pain. We didn't go to the stinkin' ER.

Jan: Well, Jim, his arm was bent back the wrong way.

Jim: There you go, taking the kids' side again.

Jan: I'm not trying to take sides with the kids. I was just hoping to get the fridge fixed in time for the graduation party next weekend.

Jim: Listen! I will get it fixed when I get it fixed! I am the man of this house, and you are supposed to do what I said. Or haven't you been reading your Bible lately?

In this story, does Jim treat Jan as number one? No, not even close. Jan's response is the right response; love, love, love. She has made Jim number one in her life.

Do You Resolve Conflict Biblically?

There will *always* be conflict in marriage. When you have two sinners who have two different mindsets, have two different personalities and were born into two different families, and are put together, there is going to be a conflict that will take place. Sometimes conflicts are over big things like money, children, sports, sex, time, habits, or family. Then there are times when conflicts are over small things, like the temperature in the house. I can remember a situation with my mother and father when my mom was experiencing a little "change" in her life for a couple of years. During this period of change, she liked the temperature of our house to be at about fifty-five degrees. My father, on the other hand, loved it about ninety-five degrees. I was in college at the time (for which I was very thankful), but when I'd come home for the holidays, I would see them go to battle with each other.

Sometimes we fight over simple things, and when we do, God calls us to go to His Word. Matthew 18 was written in regard to conflict within the church. But it can, and I believe must be, applied also to conflict in marriage. In Matthew 18:15–16, Jesus says:

> *"If your brother sins, go and show him his fault, just between the two of you. If he will listen to you, you have won your brother over. But if he will not listen, take one or two others along, so that in 'every matter may be established by the testimony of two or three witnesses.'"*

Later in that passage, Christ talked about getting the church involved as well.

If you want to resolve a conflict in marriage, there are some things to do and definitely some things not to do. If it is an issue of preference, such as the toothpaste being on the left or right side of the sink, then it is a non-issue. But if it is a bigger issue, such as finances or parenting, then I would encourage you first to give that to the Lord. Unburden your heart to God. Pray to Him. And if it is an issue of preference that is not crucial, but still a large part of your life, I would say you need to bring that before the Lord as well. He tells us to bring all our worries and concerns to Him . . . always.

If it is a sin issue, go to your husband or go to your wife, but be tenderhearted. You need to make sure you have prayed about it and you do not just jump in there like a bull in a china shop—wreaking havoc all over the place. Go to your spouse, but do it with a heart that is tender. Walk in ready to forgive. If there is a conflict that comes up and you are not ready to forgive, then you are not ready to go. And if your heart is angry, you are not ready to talk to that person. You need to pray and ask the Lord, "What do you want me to say? How do you want me to respond to my spouse?"

Go preparing to hear his or her heart. Sometimes if I have an issue with my wife, the issue is really *with me*. Before I jump into a conversation, my heart needs to be tender, I need to be ready to hear what she has to say. I need to be ready to forgive. If those things are not ready, then I *should not* go. Now, my personality is that I'm Mr. Fix-It. When there is conflict, I want to go in and fix it right away! So, boom, there is a conflict that takes place. Rather than mulling it over, thinking about it, and praying, I like to jump in with both feet. I want to fix it. But when I try to do that sometimes and things end up worse than they were at the beginning, that's because of me.

When there is conflict, first give it to the Lord. Then, speak to your spouse about the offense. If it cannot be resolved, then I would encourage you get some others involved—perhaps one of the pastors, a Sunday School teacher, the elders, or a brother or sister in Christ whom you love and respect who can come along side of you and help you.

Imagine that there is a wounded believer and he or she is lying on the ground and calling for help. What is our responsibility? Help. Pick them up. We dust them off, we point them to Christ and we say, "We are going to do this together." It is a picture of the body. It is a picture of community. In the marriage relationship, when there is conflict and you feel like it is not going anywhere, I would encourage you to get some other people involved in the process as well.

Here's what you *shouldn't* do. ATTACK! Suddenly, there is a battle zone, and cannons are blasting and bombs are exploding and it is full-scale World War Ten in your house. When you attack, nobody wins! And sometimes the philosophy is, "You hurt me, and I'm telling you what, I'm going to hurt you as long as I am alive." What has that attitude ever done to help anything or anyone? Nothing.

There are people who attack and there are those who retreat. They withdraw. The walls go up, and they give the silent treatment: "I can't talk to you right now." That is okay for a season, but five days later, when you are still trying to have a conversation with your spouse, and they say, "My mom told me when I was young, if you don't have anything nice to say, don't say it at all," that is wrong. That is the *silent treatment*. That is withdrawing. That is going backward and retreating. What that is doing is punishing your partner, and it is very, very painful. Do not retreat, do not hide, do not hole up in a wall and work and bury yourself in housework or sports or yard work or kids or ministry. Hiding is not resolving. Hiding is just avoiding the issue. When the ostrich buries his head in the sand, what's still sticking out? His entire body is still able to be seen by everyone! The ostrich thinks, *Ah, I'm safe. I can't see them, so they can't see me!* But when a predator comes along, the ostrich is torn apart.

Do not attack, do not retreat, and do not hide. Also, do not surrender. Do not become apathetic. Do not just say, "You just do what you want. You win, I give up. I do not care anymore." None of those things have ever helped resolving conflict. If you want to resolve conflict biblically, men, do your part, because God will do His. Ladies, do your part. You want to know why? Because God will do His.

> Hiding is not resolving. Hiding is just avoiding the issue.

Where Is the Peace?

The opposite of peace is war. Paul says in Romans 12:18, "If it is possible, as far as it depends on you, live at peace with *everyone*." Who does that include? Your spouse. If there is anyone whom you should strive to live at peace with, it is your spouse! Paul is saying, "Listen, I want you to pursue this. Do your part. Follow eagerly that which is peace." Whether you have been married for two weeks or you have been married seventy years, you always know conflict will come. At those times, when these conflicts arise, we are to pursue peace.

Galatians 5:22 says, "But the fruit of the Spirit is love, joy, and peace." How evident is peace in your home? How evident is peace if you have children? Do your kids see peace in your home, or do they see war? Do they see battles? What do they see?

How about your heart? Hebrews 12:14 says, "Make every effort to live in peace with everyone and to be holy." Likewise, in the Sermon on the Mount, Christ said, "Blessed are the peacemakers." Again, you might say, "Patrick, you haven't seen my house. You haven't seen what I go through. You do not see the battles I experience. No one could ever make peace out of this situation." Do you want a biblical marriage? Do your part and pray for peace. Commit to your spouse to pray for peace. This does not mean that if you pray it, you will come home every day to angels singing harmoniously in your house. This also does not mean that if you do not pray it, you will open the door and hear loud crashing sounds signaling the end of the world is imminent. Pray consistently for peace.

If your marriage is not a marriage of peace, then it will look something like this:

Jim: Oh, boy, I cannot wait for dinner tonight!

Jan: Enjoy. (Plops plate down.)

Jim: Wow, this looks pretty good, hon. Are these fresh strawberries in here? This really looks interesting.

Jan: Don't you dare insult my cooking! What do you expect when my fridge has been broken?

Jim: No, I didn't mean to insult your cooking. I was just asking if these are fresh strawberries.

Jan: Fresh? Of course they're fresh! I can't keep anything that isn't fresh in this house because I have a broken fridge. You know what? I'm ready to go out and buy some chickens just so we can have some eggs and meat around this place!

Jim: Honey, you just told me about it this morning.

Jan: And what did you do? Nothing! It went in one ear and out the other. You never listen to anything I say.

Jim: Honey, I really meant to get to it, but—

Jan: But what? Instead you chose to spend the entire day away from our home.

Jim: Well, I thought it was important to take little Bobby to the ER today.

Jan: Oh, yeah, let's talk about that little trip to the ER. How much is that going to cost us? How are we ever going to pay for that? You know, if you had a better job, we wouldn't have to pinch every single penny we had.

Jim: Hon, his arm . . . it was broken in two spots.

Jan: Oh, sure. Take his side!

Jim: No, no, honey, I'm not trying to side with the kids. And I know this refrigerator thing is important to you. I'll tell you what. I will get to it as soon as I finish this delicious strawberry meal here.

Jan: You know what? What good will that do? You couldn't fix that fridge if it started to talk and gave you step-by-step instructions.

Where's the peace? Not in that house. Does your house look like that? If you want a biblical marriage, you do your part. Jim was doing his part. He was responding in a biblical way. Some of us would have taken the strawberry meal that she had prepared and tossed it in the air, but Jim did not. His goal was to kill her with peace.

Do I Understand My Biblical Role As a Spouse?

In Ephesians 5:21–25, God talks about the role of the husband and the role of the wife. Paul writes this under the inspiration of the Holy Spirit:

> *Submit to one another out of reverence for Christ. Wives, submit yourselves to your own husbands as you do to the Lord. For the husband is the head of the wife as Christ is the head of the church, his body, of which he is the Savior. Husbands, love your wives, just as Christ loved the church and gave himself up for her.*

This is a passage that is often read at weddings, but a lot of times verse 21 is left out: "Submit to one another out of reverence for Christ." It is not a suggestion; it is a command that God gives. You do not submit out of reverence for your husband, and not out of reverence for your wife. Submit to one another out of reverence for *Christ*.

The biblical role of the wife is to submit, to follow, to affirm her husband as a leader. He is accountable to God. The role of the husband is to love, to love his wife as Christ loved the church. I pray that just about every day. I try to pray that more often with my wife, because I want her to hear that. That is a difficult task! To love my wife as Christ loved the church.

83

What did Christ ultimately do for the church? He died for the church! He gave himself up. That does not mean that if I want to be more religious then I take my life. That is not what he is saying. He is saying to love in such a way that you demonstrate your love by giving *everything*. The role of the husband is to love as Christ loved the church. It means to spend time with her, to study her, to honor her, to protect her, to pray with her.

That is the design, that is the plan and God has made that plan. Man has not created it. Can you imagine if we were the creators of marriage? The wheels would fall off that wagon before it even moved one inch! God created it! God established it! And that which God creates and establishes is good. He made the heavens and the earth, and it was good. He created man, and it was good. All these things were good. And God established the marriage relationship, and it is good.

The good news is this: Everything that God makes fits together perfectly. The role of the husband as the leader and the wife as the support fits perfectly. However, ladies, when you do not do your job the way you need to, you are at 50 percent, and 50 percent is an "F." Men, if you do not take your responsibility the way that God has intended it, then you are only halfway there, which is at 50 percent, and 50 percent is an "F." When you do that, marriage is painful. When you do that, marriage hurts. Husbands, if you do not love your wives as Christ loved the church, then your marriage is not reflecting the total image of Christ and the church. Ladies, if you are not submitting the way that God has established you to submit to his authority, you are in for a long road and a very difficult marriage.

Sometimes you'll hear this statement by a wife: "I would love to follow my husband, but he won't lead!" Ladies, you do your part despite your husband's attitude! Honor God with *your* life. You do not have to answer God for the way that your husband leads. Husbands, you need to lead. You need to lead biblically. You need to stand up and be a man. God has called men to be the head of the home, and as the head of the home, I have a responsibility, and you have a responsibility, to *lead!* Oftentimes, we'll use excuses such as, "Well, I wasn't raised a certain way" or "My parents were divorced, and I didn't have the role model of a father, so I do not have to lead." It does not matter! There are not any exceptions in the Scriptures. You *have* to lead!

God's called you to do that. Do you want a marriage to reflect Christ and the church? Be the leader of the home. Men, you might say, "My wife is like Jan serving that strawberry goulash!" Listen, do your part. God will do His. Wives, the Bible says you are to submit to your husbands as to the Lord. Whether they are leading in a biblical way or not, you are to submit to them as to the Lord.

Called from Darkness into Light

We need to take seriously the command to love our neighbor as ourselves and to love God with *everything*. We are followers of Christ. We are a part of not the kingdom of the world, but of the kingdom of God. We were called from darkness into light, and we need to reflect that in our marriages.

In the first scene, Jim is a bad person. He is arrogant, mean, and overbearing. At the very end of the conversation, he throws a reference about the Bible at Jan. Remember? "I'm the leader of the home, just in case you haven't read your Bible." That is cunning.

In the second scene, Jan is sarcastic, belittling, and mean. Her aim is to hurt her husband.

Finally, let's see what happens in this last scene when they respond to each other biblically in the midst of tension and conflict:

Jim: *Let me get this for you.*

Jan: *Thank you. Well, here's dinner.*

Jim: *Wow, this looks kind of good. Is it a new recipe?*

Jan: *Well, I did have to improvise a little bit. You know our fridge is still broken.*

Jim: *You know, I was hoping to get to that sometime tomorrow for you.*

Jan: *"Sometime?" That makes it sound like you are not really going to get to it anytime soon.*

Jim: *You know how busy I've been. I have meetings all day, and I have that appointment with Kyle at night. I just do not know when I'm going to do it.*

Jan: You know, this does not seem to be all that important to you, and it is very important to me.

Jim: No, hon, I know it needs to be done, but I've just been really busy. Especially this next couple of days, my plate's full.

Jan: Well, how about I call somebody and they come out and fix it for us then?

Jim: Oh, just with money being so tight now, I just can't see spending this money when I think I can fix this refrigerator myself for you.

Jan: Well, in the meantime, I'm borrowing fridge space from Darlene and trying to come up with recipes that do not call for eggs or milk or meat. I know it does not bother you a whole lot, but it is driving me nuts.

Jim: Okay, I kind of understand what's going on here. Let's work together on this. I'll tell you what we'll do. If I don't get to it tomorrow, why don't you go ahead and call somebody and get it fixed? Does that work out?

Jan: That works for me. Thank you.

Jim: Anytime.

(**smooch**)

Jim: I don't know about you, but I'm starving, and this smells great. So why don't we dig in?

During tension, in the midst of it, people can respond in the right way. Marriage is designed and created by God. And when it is done correctly, guess what? It fits perfectly. However, when we do not follow God's commands in Scriptures, they do not fit perfectly. Keep asking yourself these four questions:

1. Is my spouse number one?
2. Do I resolve conflict biblically?
3. Where is the peace?
4. Do I understand my biblical role as a spouse?

It is pretty simple when we realize how God has designed marriage and what He has for us.

Closing Prayer

God, thank you for your Word. Your Word is what gives us direction. Your Word, God, is what gives us hope. We come before you to ask that the marriages that you have put together would reflect your Son and the relationship that Jesus Christ has with the church. Lord, there are bumps and potholes and bruises and cracks, but rather than focusing on them, God, in our marriages, help us to focus on the gospel. Help our marriages to shine brightly for the cause of Jesus Christ. Lord, if there are some marriages that are struggling, may they seek counsel. May they seek wisdom from people who are running hard after You. May we reflect You in an incredible and a mighty way. We lay this before Your feet; we lay our marriages before Your feet. We lay this church before Your feet. We pray this in Christ's name, Amen.

February 22, 2009
Cornerstone Baptist Church

Chapter 7

FAILURE IS NOT FINAL
Lessons from the Life of Peter

Have you ever tried something, failed miserably at it, and decided, *I'm going to quit. I'm never going to do it again!*? What was it you tried? Piano? Did you start John Thompson Book One and never get any further? For some of you, you should go home and thank your parents that they didn't quit or give up on you when it came to things like riding a bike or potty training!

I can remember when I was little and my parents signed me up for baseball. This was not T-ball; this was serious, major-league, eight-year-old baseball. So I was put on a team called the Royals.

Now I lived in a little cul-de-sac, and there were about thirty of us all within four years of each other, and we played ball all the time. We loved it. We were outside every day. Video games hadn't even come out yet, so I wasn't stuck in a room looking at a screen all day playing Atari! We were always outside. I was used to playing ball and did pretty well. I did well at practice, too. But when game time came, when it was time for me to get a hit, it was a struggle! For several games, my bat never even came close to hitting the ball.

I had never experienced failure like that before, so I prayed. I wasn't a believer at that time, but I would pray, *God, make the guy hit me with the ball, because I want to get on first base!* After about three or four games of hearing, "Three strikes, you're out!" I told my mom I wanted to quit.

My mom was the ultimate optimist. She said to me, "Do you know who you are?" I thought, *Yeah, I'm the kid who's played three innings in right field, and hasn't gotten on base yet!* But she said, "You're Patrick Donovan McGoldrick!"

Well, there we go, that's going to help me! I'll just get up to bat and say to the pitcher, "I'm Patrick Donovan McGoldrick! You need to make sure the ball hits the bat, or we're going to have issues!"

She said, "Listen, you get up there and you hit that ball. You focus on that pitcher; don't listen to the people around you. Don't have rabbit ears. Get up there and hit the ball!" Rabbit ears? What was that all about? Rabbits must hear well, I guess—I didn't know!

So finally I decided the time had come for me to conquer this. The next time I got up to bat it was like time just froze. I can remember the pitcher throwing the pitch; I swung the bat and I heard this crack. I thought, *I know that wasn't my head!* And there was the ball, flying between the third baseman and the shortstop! I just stood there. I heard my mom yell, "RUN! RUN! RUN!!!" When I got to first base I thought, *This is the greatest day of my life! Miracles do happen! He didn't hit me; I actually hit the ball!*

On the way home my mom said, "Aren't you glad you didn't quit?" And of course I was glad. And you know what? I grew up to be a pretty good baseball player. I went to a big high school my freshman and sophomore years—about five thousand kids—and I made the team! I did well and I enjoyed it. But back when I was little, I did want to quit. If my parents had let me, I would have.

Think about your Christian life. Think about your walk with the Lord. There are times when things don't go well, or don't go according to your plan, and sometimes you think it's too hard and you just feel like quitting. I see all my neighbors living it up, having fun, experiencing all the world has to offer—I wonder, wouldn't it be easier to be a "regular" person and not a follower of Christ? There can be times in the Christian life when we just want to quit completely.

Peter Walks on Water

With that in mind, let's look at the life of Peter, in Matthew 14. This is right after Jesus fed five thousand people:

Immediately He made the disciples get into the boat and go before Him to the other side, while He dismissed the crowds. And after He had dismissed the crowds, He went up on the mountain by himself to pray. When evening came, He was there alone, but the boat by this time was a long way from the land, beaten by the waves, for the wind was against them. And in the fourth watch of the night He came to them, walking on the sea. But when the disciples saw him walking on the sea, they were terrified, and said, "It is a ghost!" and they cried out in fear. But immediately Jesus spoke to them, saying, "Take heart; it is I. Do not be afraid."

And Peter answered Him, "Lord, if it is you, command me to come to you on the water." He said, "Come." So Peter got out of the boat and walked on the water and came to Jesus. But when He saw the wind, He was afraid, and beginning to sink He cried out, "Lord, save me." Jesus immediately reached out His hand and took hold of him, saying to him, "O you of little faith, why did you doubt?" And when they got into the boat, the wind ceased. And those in the boat worshiped Him, saying, "Truly You are the Son of God." (Matthew 14:22–33)

As Matthew walks us through this account, we see it's not a good situation. The disciples were in the middle of a lake during a storm, and the boat was being beaten by the waves. But in verse 25, we read that Jesus came walking out to them on the lake.

Now let's just stop here for a minute. Sometimes we run through this without even thinking about it, because we've heard it so many times. But this is not an everyday occurrence. Not even for Jesus—He didn't walk on water every day! But here you have the Son of God, the Creator of the universe, who has power over His creation, walking out on the water to help his friends.

Well, when the disciples saw Jesus, they freaked out. They thought He was a ghost, and they were terrified! Now from my perspective, I think it would be fun to just walk around that boat for a long time, watching those disciples squirm . . . but what did Christ do? In verse 27 we see that Christ immediately identified Himself, and told them not to fear.

Peter said, "Lord, if it's You, can I come to You?" We know that there were other people in the boat, including possibly others who weren't disciples.

But only one of them said, "Hey, can I come out there and walk?" And it was Peter. What did Jesus say? "Sure, come on." And so he did.

The Bible says that as Peter was out on the water, he "saw the wind." We don't actually see the wind; what do we see? We see the effects of the wind. Now, a lot of us know the ending to this story, and we think, *Peter . . . can you believe it? He actually sunk. What a loser!* Peter was out on the water, he saw the effects of the wind, the water was lapping up on him, he took his focus off of Christ. But guess what? We all would've done that. And so he started to sink. When he cried out for the Lord to save him, Jesus immediately reached down, grabbed Peter, and pulled him up. Then Jesus rebuked Peter for not trusting, for his faith being very, very small.

Verse 32 says that then they climbed back into the boat . . . but how? Peter was going under, and Jesus grabbed a hold of him. I still think they were a distance away from the boat, because if Peter could have, he would have just grabbed a hold of the boat. So how did they get back in? Did Jesus carry Peter, or drag him? I believe that they probably walked back, on the water. Once they got back in the boat, the wind died down, and the people realized that Jesus was different! And they worshipped Him.

> Failure is not final. When you crash and burn in your walk with Christ, it doesn't mean that it's over.

Let's think about Peter's life. Did he make mistakes? Yeah. Did he sink? Yep. Would I have been down in the water? Yep! Would my focus have been off of Christ? No question about it. But failure is not final. When you crash and burn in your walk with Christ, it doesn't mean that it's over. On the worst days of your life, when you think you want to quit, that you want nothing to do with Christianity or ministry, don't throw in the towel. No. When we look at Peter's life, we see that he messed up over and over and over, and God still used him.

Jesus Asks the Disciples to Pray

Now let's look at Mark 14, right before the crucifixion:

And they went to a place called Gethsemane. And he said to his disciples, "Sit here while I pray." And he took with him Peter and James and John, and began to be greatly distressed and troubled. And he said to them, "My soul is very sorrowful, even to death. Remain here and watch." (Mark 14:32–34)

Jesus' ministry was obviously with the twelve disciples, but with Peter, James, and John, the relationship was different. He spent more time with them; I believe He also expected more from them. Christ gave them two commands: stay here and keep watch.

I had an opportunity to go through college and seminary. I had four years of Greek and two and a half years of Hebrew. And when you look at these two phrases, "stay here" and "keep watch," do you know what they mean in the original language? "Stay here" and "keep watch"! Jesus wanted them to stay there and to stay awake. It wasn't that difficult. Even I can figure that out, and I'm a knucklehead at times. It's not like He asked them to memorize the first five books of the Old Testament!

That's all they had to do. Jesus didn't even tell them to pray. But we see what happened when Jesus returned:

And he came and found them sleeping, and he said to Peter, "Simon, are you asleep? Could you not watch one hour?" (Mark 14:37)

Who was sleeping? "Them." We see that it's plural. But who did Jesus speak to? Peter. Now I've got to be honest: If I were Peter, I'd be saying, "But John was snoring, and James was drooling; yell at them too!" For some reason Jesus went right after Peter.

Blaming a Friend

When I was about ten years old, my dad told me to paint the backyard fence. It was a pretty big fence, and it was kind of dummy-proof to paint. You grabbed a big paintbrush, threw it into the gallon of paint, and slopped it on. My dad said, "You can get it on the grass, don't worry about it. Just have some fun; enjoy it."

So I asked if my buddy Dave Hayes could help me (he was kind of like my partner in crime). And my dad said, "Sure. Just use your head." So

Dave and I were out there, two little skinny kids in short shorts, listening to "YMCA" over and over. All of a sudden, down the middle of my back, I felt something wet. I turned around, and there was Dave, laughing like a little schoolgirl. So I dipped my paintbrush into the bucket and—*whack!*—I slapped him right across the face with red paint. A big paint fight ensued, and it was wonderful. We were having a blast.

Suddenly I heard, "PATRICK DONOVAN McGOLDRICK! Look what you've done!" I turned around, and there was my mom, looking at the house. Our house was somewhat close to the fence, and it was a cream color. But now it was cream with red polka-dots all over it! My mom said, "You wait till your father gets home!"

So Dave and I realized we had to clean it up. We went and got a hose and a couple of clean brushes . . . and about an hour later, as the side of the house was turning a nice shade of pink, we realized that oil-based paint doesn't come off without paint thinner! When my dad got home, he was not a friendly individual.

He wanted to know what in the world I was doing, so of course I said what anyone else would say: "Dave Hayes made me do it!" And you know the response: "IF DAVE HAYES JUMPED OFF THE GOLDEN GATE BRIDGE, WOULD YOU JUMP OFF IT TOO?!" Right then I would have, I was so scared!

So I imagine Peter must have been thinking, "What about these guys, Lord?" But Jesus focused on Peter. It was Peter who had told Jesus earlier, "I will not deny you." Jesus said, "Yes, you will." Peter actually argued with Jesus about that! So Jesus went up the mountain again, came back down, and what were they doing? Sleeping again. He went up again and came down a third time. What were they doing? They were sleeping. Peter failed miserably again. But in John 18, when Christ was arrested in the Garden, we see Peter's courage. He was the one who took a sword and cut of the soldier's ear! He showed that he was standing with Jesus.

God Uses Peter

Not all of Peter's life was a failure. In John 21, after Christ's resurrection, we read that the disciples were in a boat, fishing with nets but catching nothing.

Someone on shore suggested they cast on the other side of the boat. So they did, and suddenly they had almost more fish than they could handle. Once they realized it was Jesus, instead of suggesting that everyone quickly row to shore, Peter put on his outer garment and jumped into the water! He wanted to be with Jesus.

In Acts 2, it was Peter who stood up in the crowd and preached the gospel of Jesus Christ. On that day, three thousand people came to faith in Christ. Incredible! Who did God use to save three thousand people? Peter.

In Acts 4, Peter and John were thrown into prison for preaching Christ. If I were thrown into prison, I'd be angry; I'd throw a fit and whine and cry. But what did Peter do? Filled with the Spirit, he made this statement to his captors:

"This Jesus is the stone that was rejected by you, the builders, which has become the cornerstone. And there is salvation in no one else, for there is no other name under heaven given among men by which we must be saved." (Acts 4:12)

It was all about Christ! In Acts 5, when the apostles were told by the religious leaders to stop preaching Christ, Peter and the other apostles said, "We're going to obey God rather than men." I bet that went over really, really well!

So when you look at Peter's life, don't look at it as a failure. Look at it as a guy who is like you and me—a guy who made mistakes but sought forgiveness and was used by God. You will make mistakes. You will sin. You will openly rebel. But you will seek forgiveness, and you will move forward. History tells us that as Peter was being crucified, he asked that the cross be turned upside down, because he didn't feel worthy enough to be crucified in the same way as his Savior.

I tell you this to encourage you. The greatest thing you could ever do is to remain close to the Lord and to run hard after Jesus Christ. Surround yourself with godly people who will love you, care for you, and never give up on you—because God loves you and cares for you and won't give up on you. He is relentless in His pursuit of you.

August 30, 2011
Baptist Bible College

Chapter 8

GOD COMMANDS AND JONAH RUNS
Jonah 1

Do you believe in a God who spoke the universe into being? Who develops a relationship with people? Who loves His children? Who draws His children to Himself? Who will never, ever let His children go? This is the message of Jonah.

Many times when we open up the book of Jonah, we take out a big baseball bat and we slug away at this guy. We say, "How could you not listen to God's voice, when He said to you, 'I want you to go. I want you to talk to Nineveh. I want you to preach repentance'? How could you refuse?"

But focus your attention for a moment on people you find difficult to love. You might see specific faces, or you might be thinking of certain types of people, people groups or personalities. Often we dismiss these people or have little contact with them because of what they do, or what they say, or how they act. Sometimes we even see them as enemies.

Now, imagine that one of those people, or one of those groups of people, became anti-God. Suddenly we feel justified thinking of these people as enemies, because now they don't agree with us theologically or biblically. That's what Jonah went through.

The book of Jonah has been attacked more than any other of the Old Testament prophets. A lot of people cannot wrap their minds around the fact that God prepared a fish big enough to swallow Jonah and for Jonah to be able to live inside that fish for three days and three nights. They say, "We just don't have enough faith in it."

Let me tell you what: Scripture is a *supernatural* book, about *supernatural* things, about a *supernatural* God who is interested in us. Either it is *all* right, or it is *all* a joke. And it is *all* right!

Background

Jonah was a prophet to Israel; he spoke directly to God's people. The book of Jonah was written eight centuries before the birth of Jesus Christ, and Jonah is one of only four prophets whose ministry Christ mentioned while on earth.

What would you say is the theme of the book of Jonah? A fish? Nineveh? Jonah himself? The word *fish* is used four times in the book. *Nineveh* is used nine times. *Jonah* shows up eighteen times. But God's name shows up thirty-eight times in a book of only forty verses! *God* is the theme of this book: God's message, God's plan. As you read, you begin to see: "And the Lord . . . ," "Then the Lord . . . ," "And then God . . ."

Overview

Chapter 1: God calls Jonah to preach to Nineveh. Jonah refuses to go, gets in a ship, and goes the opposite direction. God sends a storm—it's a big storm—and sailors toss Jonah overboard. God prepares a fish to swallow Jonah.

Chapter 2: In the belly of a fish, after rebelling against the Creator of the universe, Jonah gets right with God. The fish spits him out (that had to have been a lovely sight).

Chapter 3: Jonah obeys God. He goes to Nineveh. He preaches, and there is a revival like none other. From the top dog to the bottom person, people give their hearts to the Creator.

Chapter 4: Jonah is angry with God. Instead of throwing a revival party, he throws a pity party.

The Message of Jonah

I want to make two statements about the book of Jonah that are implied over and over within the text. The first one is this: *The longer our rebellion lasts, the harder it is to get back to God.* Rebellion is not ignorance. Rebellion is when you know what God wants you to do, but you put your finger in His face and say, "I will not do it!"

The second thing is this: *God is relentless in His pursuit of us.* God is a very loving, merciful, caring, patient and pursuing God. And when He lays His hand on your life—let me tell you what—it is for your good. You can run, you can

> The longer our rebellion lasts, the harder it is to get back to God.

hide, you can fight, and you can struggle . . . but when you do, you need to realize this: God is coming after you! If you are His child, He's not going to let you go. He will not blink, and He will come after you. He will be relentless.

Modern-Day Jonah

In the book of Jonah, there is a giant fish, a boat, and a prophet. That can be pretty hard for us to relate today. But what would a modern Jonah look like, living in our world in the twenty-first century? Here's one possibility:

I started a new job a while back. It was really a perfect opportunity for me, and I was so pumped to get it. Of course I wanted to make a good first impression—not only with my boss, but also with the guys I worked with. They seemed pretty cool and were nice enough, but they were a little intimidating. And I've got to admit, I hadn't really thought or prayed about how my faith should be a part of my new workplace. I just wanted to be accepted and to fit in.

But about a week into my new job, I heard a sermon about living for God in every area of my life. The pastor talked about how who I am at church on Sunday should be the same guy that I am on Monday at work. He talked about being a light for Christ in the workplace. I tell you what, it was pretty convicting. I mean, it's not like I was being a totally different person at work. But I definitely wasn't advertising the fact that I was a Christian.

I felt so uncomfortable sitting in church that day. It was like God was speaking directly to me, telling me to speak up for Him that week at work. But I didn't know what to do. Should I walk into work and say, "Hey! Do you know Jesus?" I just started pushing away the thoughts. I didn't want to admit that God was trying to tell me something.

I didn't think about it again until the next day. One of the guys brought up something about church or religion. He was mad about a situation and was ranting about how religious people are all just a bunch of hypocrites. I got this feeling in the pit of my stomach. I knew God was telling me to stand up for Him . . . but I just didn't want to. I didn't want to risk it. I wasn't sure when to speak up or what to say. But then the guy looked directly at me and said, "Am I right, or what?" Boom! There it was—my perfect opportunity. But all I said was, "Yeah, man, you're right."

The next day another guy started talking about some girl at work, and it quickly turned totally offensive. I knew it wasn't right, but I didn't know what to say. The other guys were laughing and joining in. Being the new guy, I didn't want to ruffle anyone's feathers. So I just kind of smiled and laughed.

From there it just started to snowball. Not only did I find myself continuing to laugh at the things they said, but I started joining in. And every time, I felt myself falling deeper and deeper into a pit.

Then came the time we had messed up on a project, and we were going to get chewed out by our boss. But one of the guys made up a story to get around it. Everyone agreed to go along with it. I didn't want to, but what else was I supposed to do? When the boss called me in, I sat there and lied straight to his face. I left his office feeling sick to my stomach. I knew I should go back in and tell him the truth. I knew God wanted me to make it right. But again, I just came up with excuses and found a way to justify what I had done. Day after day I ignored His voice.

Then came the day I did something I never thought I would do. We were offsite working on a project, and a couple of my buddies had this great idea to go golfing instead of finishing the job. It was really the perfect scenario, so they said: We were ahead of schedule and far away from anyone we knew. No one would ever find out. I had never stood up to them before, and there was no way I could start now. So off I went. We used the company vehicle, the company's fuel, the company's time.

The trouble is, this time our boss did find out. He found out about everything, including all the lies we had told. I lost my job that day. I went home and just sat on the couch for the longest time, wondering how I had gotten myself in this mess. I called myself a Christian, and God had blessed me with an amazing job. Yet I found myself sitting on my couch in the middle of the day, unemployed, a liar and a thief. How did it come to this? I thought that obeying God would cost me too much. So instead I ran from Him and ended up paying a much higher price.

That would be a Jonah in today's world. And just like in Jonah's day, the rebellion cost much, much too high a price.

Jonah's Assignment

The word of the Lord came to Jonah the son of Amittai: "Go to the great city of Nineveh and preach against it, because its wickedness has come up before me." (Jonah 1:1–2)

God was speaking *directly to* Jonah. Now, when I was growing up, my dad would say things directly to me, like, "Go cut the grass," and I would say, "No, I don't want to." We would get into a discussion about it, and he would say, "What part of 'go cut the grass' do you not understand?" I didn't have an answer. I always hated not having an answer!

Now let me ask you a question: When you look this passage in Jonah, is it a *suggestion* or is it a *command*? It is a command. Is there anything fuzzy or confusing about "Go and preach?" Absolutely not! We like a little wiggle room, but God clearly says, "GO." There's nothing about "GO!" that Jonah didn't understand.

In fact, Jonah understood all too well. The last place on earth he wanted to go was Nineveh, yet his assignment was to go to this wicked city and tell the people, "Repent! Because if you don't, there will be consequences!" He was told to go and confront their sin. Jonah was told to do what John the Baptist did. John the Baptist stood up for truth—and it got him killed.

Jonah's Response

Verse 3 starts with, "But Jonah . . ." That word "but" gets so many people in trouble—in trouble with parents, in trouble with family, in trouble with friends, in trouble with employers, in trouble with God.

But Jonah ran away from the Lord and headed for Tarshish. He went down to Joppa, where he found a ship bound for that port. After paying the fare, he went aboard and sailed for Tarshish to flee from the Lord. (1:3)

Now, Tarshish and Nineveh are not neighbors. God told Jonah to go northeast, but Jonah went south and then headed west. It says he "found" a ship bound for that port. Isn't that interesting? He just "happened" to find a ship going in the opposite direction. If you want to rebel against God, you *will* find a way. Jonah wanted to get as far away from Nineveh as he could, as quickly as he could. He wanted no part of God's instruction to him.

Steps of Rebellion

Every step of rebellion gets you farther and farther away from God. Remember our modern-day Jonah? His rebellion began with a little smile and a little laugh, seemingly harmless at first. But that first little step led to bigger and bigger steps. Your rebellion may start with a day, and then it becomes a week. Then it's a month, then it's a year . . . and soon that rebellion becomes a habit and a lifetime.

If you've seen children learning how to walk, you know those first couple of steps are great. They get one or two steps, and then they fall down! But then they start to get one, two, three, four, five steps, then a dozen, and before long, you start to wish they'd never learned to walk! When they're first walking, it starts small—but with each step, they get better and better and start walking farther and farther. In the same way, every step of rebellion gets you farther and farther away from the Lord.

Once Jonah made that first step to the south, it was harder to turn around and do the right thing. When I let my eyes wander to the wrong place, it's hard to put my focus back to the cross and what Christ has done. When I allow my mind to think the wrong thing, it is so hard to turn it around and think truth. The best advice: Don't go there in the first place!

You may say, "Well, Patrick, that is easier said than done!" I know that. And every single day, I struggle with it. When I get up in the morning, it's not my first instinct to say, "Well, good morning, Lord! Thank you for that rest! I feel so refreshed!" No, it is a struggle, and I have to beat myself up. I have to make myself a slave to my Savior, compared to a slave to sin.

Verse 3 tells us that Jonah *ran away* from the Lord. It was blatant disregard for God. When you rebel against God, you find your feet taking you places you shouldn't go. You find your mind wandering in places it shouldn't be. You find

> Your rebellion may start with a day, and then it becomes a week. Then it's a month, then it's a year . . . and soon that rebellion becomes a habit and a lifetime.

your eyes watching things that they shouldn't watch. And for Jonah, it was a step, then another step, and another step, and pretty soon he started gaining ground, moving fast. And then it was to the point that he was no longer walking. He was *running* from the Lord.

Futility of Running from God

Two hundred years before Jonah, David wrote Psalm 139. Let's look at some verses from this Psalm, keeping in mind that Jonah was trying to *get away from God:*

> *Where can I go from your Spirit?*
> *Where can I flee from your presence?*

103

If I go up to the heavens, you are there;
if I make my bed in the depths, you are there.
If I rise on the wings of the dawn,
if I settle on the far side of the sea,
even there your hand will guide me,
your right hand will hold me fast. (Psalm 139:7–10)

Where is God? He is everywhere. Yet Jonah was trying to run from Him. Most likely, Jonah knew Psalm 139. But because of his sin, because of the deceitfulness of his own heart, he thought he could get away from God. When we rebel, we harden our hearts to the truths we know. Our thinking gets so messed up that we believe we can do things that we absolutely cannot do. We become blind; we no longer listen to the Spirit of God.

Nineveh

So why didn't Jonah want to go to Nineveh? Was it the climate? Was it a poor exchange rate? Was their housing market in a slump? No. Nineveh was the capitol of the Assyrian empire and an enemy of Israel. The Assyrians were a cruel, ruthless and heartless people. One thing they were known for was skinning people alive. Does that give you an idea of why Jonah wouldn't want to go there?

At the end of the book, we learn that Jonah knew God would have mercy on the Ninevites. Jonah didn't want them to repent. He *wanted* to see the destruction of Nineveh, because he hated them. And Jonah's response was so completely contrary to the response of Jesus Christ. Who did Jesus Christ have dinner with? Tax collectors and sinners. Christ was not exclusive to one type of person or one group of people; His ministry was to the multitudes.

God's Relentless Pursuit

Then the Lord sent a great wind on the sea, and such a violent storm
arose that the ship threatened to break up. All the sailors were afraid

and each cried out to his own god. And they threw the cargo into the sea to lighten the ship. (Jonah 1:4–5)

Now we see God's pursuit! Jonah was going a different direction, and God said, "I'm going after him." God was about to let Jonah know who He was. He sent a storm, and it was a *serious* storm! God sent a storm that was so violent, the sailors were afraid. That's like a taxi driver being nervous in rush hour! So what did they do? They cried out to their own gods. They were starting to get desperate.

Then they decided to throw the cargo into the sea. Now, that's *really* desperate! You have to remember that the cargo is their food, their water, maybe even their clothes. Possibly it was a shipment they were delivering to another city. I guess their philosophy was, "I'd rather be alive without a job than dead with a job. Let's just get rid of everything!"

But Jonah had gone below deck, where he lay down and fell into a deep sleep. The captain went to him and said, "How can you sleep? Get up and call on your god! Maybe he will take notice of us so that we will not perish." Then the sailors said to each other, "Come, let us cast lots to find out who is responsible for this calamity." They cast lots and the lot fell on Jonah. (1:5b–7)

You've got to imagine that at the point they started casting lots, Jonah was thinking, *Oh man, I'm going to pull out my rabbit's foot. I'm going to cross my fingers, toes, arms, and legs and hope that lot does not fall on me!*

Where was Jonah in the beginning? He was asleep. Now, I've heard of heavy sleepers, but the ship was going up and down, so much that the sailors were crying out in fear. And yet Jonah was down below, nestled up with a blankie and a pillow, sawing logs! He was *out*. The captain went down and got right in his face: "Call on *your* god; ours didn't work!" The captain knew the severity of the situation, yet Jonah did not call on God at that point.

So they asked him, "Tell us, who is responsible for making all this trouble for us? What kind of work do you do? Where do you come from? What is your country? From what people are you?" (1:8)

The sailors began to grill him, and Jonah didn't answer vaguely. Look at what he said:

"I am a Hebrew and I worship the Lord, the God of heaven, who made the sea and the dry land." (1:9)

Ooh, a little contradiction there, because Jonah really wasn't worshiping God. He was only *acknowledging* God. And the response of the sailors again:

This terrified them and they asked, "What have you done?" (They knew he was running away from the Lord, because he had already told them so.) (1:10)

They were terrified because they understood the God of Israel. They understood the God of Abraham, Isaac and Jacob. They'd heard the stories of David; they knew the story of the Red Sea; and they wanted to know, "What have you done?"

Why would someone run from God? Why would someone run from our Savior, Jesus Christ, who has nothing but our best interest in mind, and who loves us and cares for us?

Jonah Overboard

The sea was getting rougher and rougher. So they asked him, "What should we do to you to make the sea calm down for us?" (1:11)

Isn't that a nice way to ask? When you think of sailors, phrases like "drunken sailors" or "swearing like a sailor" might come to mind. You probably don't think of them as people with lots of compassion! Yet they asked Jonah what they should do to him.

The sea was growing rougher and rougher, and Jonah was not getting the message, so God turned up the heat. It's as if God was saying, "You think *that* was bad? Well, I'm going to *keep* coming after you, and I'm not going to let up. When you sleep, I'm going to invade your dreams. When you're awake, I'm going to invade your thoughts. And I want you to know that every step you take, I am after you!"

Now for some of us, we say, "Hallelujah, I *love* that promise!" But for me at times, I say, "Argh, that is scary!" On the one hand, I like knowing that I can't run, I can't hide, and I can't get anywhere from God. But on the other hand, sometimes I want to do things that God won't see, or I want to respond in a way that God won't hear. But that could never happen!

"Pick me up and throw me into the sea," he replied, "and it will become calm. I know that it is my fault that this great storm has come upon you." (1:12)

Some of us may look at Jonah's answer and think that it's a noble response—but it's not. Jonah should have said, "Give me a moment." He should have fallen to his knees right there, waved the white flag and said to God, "Forgive me. I have been running from you. I will do what you want me to do."

Of course I can't be sure, but I imagine that if Jonah had dropped to his knees and said that to the Lord, the sea would have grown calm. But Jonah didn't do that. He basically said, "I would rather die than go and preach to those people at Nineveh."

How does this happen? Jonah was God's prophet, yet he was saying in the face of God, "I will not do what you want me to do!" How did he get to this place? One step at a time. Jonah ran away; he got on a boat; and he was where he shouldn't be. A storm came up. He could have dropped to his knees and asked for forgiveness, but he didn't. He told them to throw him overboard.

Instead, the men did their best to row back to land. But they could not, for the sea grew even wilder than before. (1:13)

These guys are great—these are the kind of sailors I would like! They seem like wonderful people! Instead of throwing Jonah overboard, these guys were trying to save his life. The men did their best to row to land, but they couldn't because the sea grew even wilder than before.

Verse 4 says it's a "violent storm." Verse 11 says, "rougher and rougher." Verse 13 says, "The sea grew wilder than before." The longer he was on that boat, the worse the ocean was going to become. And the sailors were trying to row to shore, but who were they rowing against? God. They were going to lose, and God was going to win.

> Sometimes I want to do things that God won't see, or I want to respond in a way that God won't hear.

It reminds me of Peter, one of my favorite characters in the New Testament. Peter said to Jesus, "I will stand with you to the point of death!" Jesus said, "No, you're going to deny me." Peter: "No, I'm not!" Jesus: "Yes, you're going to deny me." And we know that he did. Every time you argue against God, you will lose.

Then they cried out to the Lord, "Please, Lord, do not let us die for taking this man's life. Do not hold us accountable for killing an innocent man, for you, Lord, have done as you pleased." (1:14)

Finally, *someone* cried out to God, but it wasn't Jonah—it was the sailors! They were talking to Yahweh, the Creator of the seas and the land. They didn't really know what else to do. They'd called out to their gods, they'd "rubbed their rabbit's foot," and they'd thrown their stuff overboard. Now they were talking to God, maybe for the first time in their lives.

God at Work Through Jonah's Sin

Then they took Jonah and they threw him overboard and the raging sea grew calm. At this the men greatly feared the Lord, and they offered a sacrifice to the Lord and made vows to him. (1:15–16)

Jonah's trip was to go northeast. Instead, he rebelled against God. He ended up in a boat with pagan sailors who were calling out to their own gods. What happened to these sailors? Their lives were transformed. They threw Jonah overboard, the seas grew calm, and they worshiped God. They feared the Lord. I believe these sailors were transformed due to the disobedience of Jonah.

I don't say this to encourage you to be disobedient! Don't excuse your disobedience because you know God can still use you; that's wrong thinking. I say this to remind you that whether we obey God or not, His plans will not be defeated. He works out His will in spite of our sin.

A Lonely Place

So where was Jonah? He was now in the sea, fighting for his life. What would he do out in the middle of the sea? He could only stay afloat for so long. His arms were going to get tired. Maybe it was cold.

I've been through lonely places in my life and in my spiritual walk. They are difficult, hard times. I don't like it. Sometimes it is due to my own sin and stupidity, and sometimes it's because God has me out in the wilderness for a while. I want you to imagine Jonah out there. The end of the chapter talks about how God prepared a fish and sent it to swallow Jonah. This story goes from good (the Word of God coming to Jonah) to bad (him running from God), to worse (him floating in the sea about to get swallowed by a fish). So what do you do with this? How do you process this through your mind?

You may hope for a funny story to end with so you can feel happy and smiley! But I have no good news for you, other than one word: repent! I don't have a cute story or illustration. But I do want to challenge you to wave the white flag—because if you don't, you will lose.

For some of you, maybe it's a habit that you're just not giving over to the Lord. Or maybe it's a pattern in your life that you aren't giving over to the gospel. Maybe it's a relationship that's gone bad. You know what you need to do? You need to wave the white flag. If you don't, you are going to lose!

Maybe it's a level of commitment. Maybe it's getting baptized. Maybe you need to be serving. You know what you need to do? You need to wave the white flag. If you don't, you are going to lose!

Maybe you're not passionate about God. Maybe you're having trouble loving God. Maybe you don't *want* to love God. Maybe it's your marriage. Maybe you won't allow your husband to lead your family, or you won't love your wife as Christ loved the church. Maybe your relationships with your kids have gone bad. You know what you need to do? You need to wave the white flag. If you don't, you are going to lose!

Maybe it's your thoughts. *Whatever* it is—fill in the blank—if you don't surrender, you will lose. How easy is it to wave the white flag? Sometimes it's really difficult. Sometimes I'd like to dig a hole and bury the flag in it because I would rather fight than give in. But if I do, I will lose.

I would encourage you, wherever you are in your walk with Christ, surrender your heart to Him. I think until I take my last breath, I need to keep waving that white flag.

July 19, 2009
Cornerstone Baptist Church

Chapter 9

GOD PURSUES, JONAH PRAYS, GOD ANSWERS!
Jonah 2

When I was a junior in college, I was attending a Bible school of about six hundred students. I was on the soccer team, and we were scheduled to play a scrimmage against State University of New York (SUNY). SUNY has a few larger campuses and several little ones all throughout the state. When the school scheduled this scrimmage, we were under the impression that we were going to take on one of the schools with approximately six or seven hundred students. But on that day, when we pulled up to the campus, we realized we were at a "Mack Daddy" of SUNY—one of the major campuses of State University of New York!

We got out of our vans and walked onto this plush, gorgeous field—a field like I had never seen before in my life. I looked around at the guys on the other team, and I thought, *Wow, they're big! They're so fast! They're so strong!* And I'm sure you can imagine the rest! By half time, the score was 17-0.

Our coach went over to the sideline and said to the other coach, "Look, I'm sorry, but we are in two different leagues; we're just going to forfeit the game right now." (This was before they had the "mercy rule.") Then our coach pulled us together and said, "We're done. We're ending the game right now, because if we don't, guess what? It's only going to get worse."

Now, I'm an optimist, but I knew he was right! We had barely touched the ball. The other team was even being gracious enough to kick the ball out of bounds to give us some type of chance! Every once in a while you've just got to say, "I surrender, no more."

111

Life Inside a Fish

In Jonah 1, we saw the prophet Jonah running from God, refusing to surrender. But God pursued Jonah, and we left him at the end of the last chapter bobbing up and down in the sea. Look now at verse 17:

> *Now the LORD provided a huge fish to swallow Jonah, and Jonah was in the belly of the fish three days and three nights. (Jonah 1:17 ESV)*

I like the translation of the NASB: "And the LORD appointed a great fish . . ." Jonah had an appointment, set up by God, with a fish! I know people struggle with that idea—but if God can create everything out of nothing, He can set up an appointment with a fish! That fish was no accident.

The temperature inside the belly of a fish is between 108 and 115 degrees; there are gastric juices all over the place. It's not a place where you want to buy real estate! Yet this is where Jonah lived for three days.

> God wants our attention as well. God would rather have us live anywhere than live in disobedience to Him.

I think you would agree that sending a fish to swallow Jonah was pretty radical! Why did God do something so radical to get Jonah's attention? Well remember, first God spoke gently to Jonah and told him to go to Nineveh. When Jonah didn't obey, God aggressively pursued him on the ship and sent a storm. Jonah still didn't respond, so God increased the severity of the storm. Still no repentance from Jonah. Yet God was relentless; finally He used the radical means of a giant fish to get Jonah's attention.

God wants our attention as well. God would rather have us live anywhere than live in disobedience to Him. So if it's going to take a fish, He will use a fish! God will get His point across. Nothing is too radical for God when He is getting a hold of His people.

Is It Really True?

Some people ask, "How can a man survive in the belly of a fish three days and three nights?" They don't believe it's true. Some write it off as merely a parable—a story illustrating a religious truth or spiritual lesson. Christ often spoke in parables, but listen to what He said in Matthew 12, after the Pharisees asked for a "sign":

> But he answered them, "An evil and adulterous generation seeks for a sign, but no sign will be given to it except the sign of the prophet Jonah. For just as Jonah was three days and three nights in the belly of the great fish, so will the Son of Man be three days and three nights in the heart of the earth. The men of Nineveh will rise up at the judgment with this generation and condemn it, for they repented at the preaching of Jonah, and behold, something greater than Jonah is here." (Matthew 12:39–41 ESV)

Who is that "something greater"? It's Christ. And here Jesus Christ talks about Jonah and the great fish not as a parable, but as a historical event—a sign given by God.

John Piper said this: "Those of us who respect the wisdom of Christ will be very slow to call His judgment into question." Here's Patrick's paraphrase: "If it's good enough for Jesus, it's good enough for me!" Why would we question Christ? The story of Jonah is a literal story.

So to answer the question, How can a man survive . . . ? The answer is he can't, just as no person can stay three days and three nights in the heart of the earth—dead—and then come back to life again. Jesus knew that this was no ordinary event. It was a miraculous sign of God's graciousness and His powerful intervention. There's no point in trying to explain it scientifically any more than there is reason to try to scientifically explain the miracles of Christ.

Jonah's Prayer

> "I called out to the LORD, out of my distress, and he answered me; out of the belly of Sheol I cried, and you heard my voice. For you cast me into the deep, into the heart of the seas, and the flood surrounded me; all your waves and your billows passed over me. Then I said, 'I am driven away from your sight; yet I shall again look upon your holy

temple.' The waters closed in over me to take my life; the deep sur-rounded me; weeds were wrapped about my head at the roots of the mountains. I went down to the land whose bars closed upon me forever; yet you brought up my life from the pit, O LORD my God. When my life was fainting away, I remembered the LORD, and my prayer came to you, into your holy temple. Those who pay regard to vain idols forsake their hope of steadfast love. But I with the voice of thanksgiving will sacrifice to you; what I have vowed I will pay. Salvation belongs to the LORD!" (Jonah 2:2–9 ESV)

From inside the fish, Jonah prayed to the Lord his God. When Jonah prayed about his "distress," he was talking about the threat of the water. Humanly speaking, he couldn't live out there for a long period of time; the fish became his salvation.

This whole passage gives us insight on how and why God answers prayer when we call on Him in distress. Have you ever been at a point in your life when things weren't going according to your plan? Maybe you were living in disobedience, maybe you were running from God, or maybe it was some-thing completely out of your control. Did you ever just cry out and say, *God, save me! God, help me! I don't know what to do here!* That is what Jonah did in this chapter. This prayer can be an encouragement to us as we see that God does answer our prayers.

Ways in Which God Answers

Let's take a look at some of the different ways God answers us, based on Jonah's prayer.

God Answers in Spite of Our Guilt

"I called out to the LORD, out of my distress, and he answered me." (2:2 ESV)

Now remember this: Jonah was not on his way to Nineveh when this took place. He was actually running from God; he was guilty of disobedi-ence. Often when we are guilty of disobedience, we think, *Before I cry out* to God, *I need to clean myself up. I need to get some things in order.* But Jonah cries out in his distress. In this passage God shows us that He listened to Jonah's prayer even though Jonah hadn't yet cleaned himself up!

Jonah's prayer can be described as a psalm, and it's very similar to the prayers we see in the book of Psalms. In Psalm 107:10–16, the author says,

> *Some sat in darkness and in the shadow of death, prisoners in affliction and in irons, for they had rebelled against the words of God, and spurned the counsel of the Most High. So he bowed their hearts down with hard labor; they fell down, with none to help. Then they cried to the Lord in their trouble, and he delivered them from their distress. He brought them out of darkness and the shadow of death, and burst their bonds apart. Let them thank the LORD for his steadfast love, for his wondrous works to the children of man! For he shatters the doors of bronze and cuts in two the bars of iron. (Psalm 107:10–16 ESV)*

Think about this passage: it portrays for us deepest gloom—prisoners suffering in iron chains because they have not listened to the counsel of God. This is not a pretty picture. But they cried to the Lord in their trouble, and what happened? God saved them! God is in the business of saving people. And when He does it, He receives the glory and we receive such encouragement to see Him change lives.

It's very similar to what Jonah experienced. This Psalm doesn't say, "First they cleaned up." No. In their distress, they cried out to God. It is the same for us. God isn't saying, "You need to clean up. You need to act this way. You need to cut your hair, you need to wear a tie . . ." He's telling us to cry out to Him, *God, I don't know what to do, and so I am just placing my life here on the altar, saying that I need Your help!*

God Answers in Spite of His Judgment

> *"For you cast me into the deep, into the heart of the seas, and the flood surrounded me; all your waves and your billows passed over me. Then I said, 'I am driven away from your sight; yet I shall again look upon your holy temple.'" (Jonah 2:3–4 ESV)*

Who threw Jonah into the water? In Jonah 1:15 we read that the sailors threw Jonah overboard! Yet here in chapter 2, Jonah said that God cast him into the sea. The sailors physically threw him over, but Jonah knew that ultimately it was God. God used those sailors to carry out judgment on Jonah.

> There will be times in our lives that we feel the hand of God pressing against us in discipline. But it's at that moment, when we feel the conviction of the Spirit of God, that we should say, "God, save me!"

Sometimes people say, "God put me here because of my sin, and there's no point in praying." Yet Jonah does pray to the one who put him there. Was God judging Jonah? Yes—and rightly so. There will be times in our lives that we feel the hand of God pressing against us in discipline. But it's at that moment, when we feel the conviction of the Spirit of God, that we should say, "God, save me! God, help me!"

"The waters closed in over me to take my life; the deep surrounded me; weeds were wrapped about my head at the roots of the mountains. I went down to the land whose bars closed upon me forever; yet you brought up my life from the pit, O LORD MY GOD." (2:5–6 ESV)

Now this was not your typical "bad day"! Jonah was in a mess of judgment when he cried out to God. And notice Jonah didn't fight with God; he didn't try to reason it out with the Lord. He didn't try to sell something to God. And what did God do? Ultimately, He saved Jonah.

God Answers "In the Nick of Time," in Ways We Don't Expect

"When my life was fainting away, I remembered the LORD, and my prayer came to you, into your holy temple." (2:7 ESV)

The term "fainting away" means losing consciousness. He was in, and he was out—and who did he remember? His mother? His friends? His accountability partner? No! He remembered the Lord! And we see through the rest of the book that Jonah's prayer rose to God. What a demonstration of God's grace and mercy!

Often God demonstrates His grace and mercy in ways we don't expect. Jonah certainly didn't ask to be swallowed by a fish! The fish's belly doesn't at first glance seem like God's grace, does it? It's bad out there—but whoa! It's not too good in here either! Yet Jonah knew that God used this fish to save him. He didn't complain about the smelly, slimy surroundings; he knew that a fish's belly is better than the bottom of the ocean, with seaweed wrapped around his head, not breathing anymore!

God Answers to Show Us Who He Is

"Those who pay regard to vain idols forsake their hope of steadfast love. But I with the voice of thanksgiving will sacrifice to you; what I have vowed I will pay. Salvation belongs to the LORD!" (2:8–9 ESV)

What a great contrast here in this passage! Jonah knew that when we cling to worthless idols, we forfeit the grace that could be ours. So instead, with a song of thanksgiving, he sacrificed to God.

When the storm started and Jonah was in the bottom of the boat, the sailors were up on top, frantically throwing things overboard and calling on their gods, with no success. And then we saw Jonah preaching to himself: *Why would I follow those worthless idols, when I have a relationship with the Creator of the universe?* Jonah knew that if you leave God, you leave mercy. And then God filled his heart with thanksgiving.

" and call upon me in the day of trouble; I will deliver you, and you shall glorify me." (Psalm 50:15 ESV)

Again, in this Psalm, we see such a contrast between worthless idols and a relationship with the Creator.

Every once in a while, when I was growing up, I would try to show my father who I was by getting into a little argument. I'd stick my chest out, all tough and proud, and he would say to me, "Do you know who I am? Let me tell you something, young man: I brought you into this world, and I can take you out!" My parents would frequently remind me who I was and who they were.

Think about that in relation to God and Jonah. God kept reminding Jonah, "This is who I am," yet Jonah kept putting his fist up in the air. So God got Jonah's attention in other ways—ultimately by sending a fish to swallow Jonah. And when God answered Jonah's prayer, He showed again who He was . . . not only a God of power and judgment, but a God of mercy and grace.

Surrender and Deliverance

And the LORD spoke to the fish, and it vomited Jonah out upon the dry land. (Jonah 2:10 ESV)

Who created the sea? Who created the fish? Who created the land? It's all God. And when Jonah finally threw his arms up in the air and said, *I surrender! I'm done!* God delivered him from the fish. Not a real soft, comfy, cozy ending there, is it? No red carpet. Yet God delivered Jonah.

What about us? We need to throw our arms up in the air every day and say, *God, I surrender.* Because God will do whatever it takes to get our attention. And if we claim the name of Christ, God's desire for us is to live in obedience to Him. If we choose to disobey, we will find ourselves fighting a battle we can never win.

Let this be the prayer and the passion of our hearts—that we would surrender our lives to the cross daily.

August 9, 2009
Cornerstone Baptist Church

Chapter 10

JONAH OBEYS, NINEVEH REPENTS, GOD RELENTS!
Jonah 3

Then the word of the LORD came to Jonah a second time: "Go to the great city of Nineveh and proclaim to it the message I give you." Jonah obeyed the word of the LORD and went to Nineveh. Now Nineveh was a very important city—a visit required three days. On the first day, Jonah started into the city. He proclaimed: "Forty more days and Nineveh will be overturned." (Jonah 3:1–4)

In the beginning of the book of Jonah, God called Jonah a first time to go to Nineveh, and Jonah refused. God then gave Jonah a second chance and showed him grace and another opportunity to follow Him in obedience. The first call is recorded in Jonah 1:2; the second in Jonah 3:2. In chapter 1, it says, "Go to that great city of Nineveh and preach against it because its wickedness has come up before me." However, in chapter 3, God's call was changed: "Go to the great city of Nineveh and proclaim to it the message I give you."

Nineveh Is a Huge City

There are some similarities between the two passages. First, God called it a great city. Let me define the word *great* for you. God was not saying, "Jonah, this is a great place for you to go to. You think that Disney World is great? Just wait until you go meet some of those Ninevites."

119

Rather, the word *great* meant that it was a very large city. The walls around the city were about one hundred feet high. Not only were the walls one hundred feet high, they were also extremely wide. The width of the walls could hold three chariots side-by-side. That is pretty big. They also had fifteen hundred towers, each of which was two hundred feet high. This may cause you to ask the question, "Why would they want to build something so big?" The answer is that Nineveh was a country of war. They built this great, big, massive city because they made a lot of enemies who wanted to destroy them. This was the city that God called Jonah to go to.

Also do not forget the people of Nineveh. Do you remember the first time Jonah said no to God? It was after God told Jonah, "I want you to go to a people that are not Mine, and I want you to preach to them about their wickedness." Part of Jonah's apprehension was because they were not God's people. They were what we would call Gentiles. Nothing good ever took place in Nineveh. And this was because of the Ninevites.

Nonetheless, God called Jonah to go preach to the Ninevites. He said, "Their wickedness has come up before me." Then later, in chapter 3, He said, "Proclaim to [them] the message I give you." God was saying, "I want you to go to Nineveh, and I want you to preach. I'm not going to tell you what to say until you get there. I want you to go by faith, and once you get there, I will tell you what you must preach."

Eventually, Jonah obeyed God and went to Nineveh. I personally do not believe that the reason Jonah finally relented and went to Nineveh was because he was excited about sharing God's grace. It wasn't because he had a passion for the Ninevites. No, rather it was because he spent three nights in the belly of a fish. When Jonah did not obey, there were consequences—there was disaster. He did not go because he cared about them (we will see this in Jonah 4). He did it because he had to.

After being punished when I was a little kid, my mom would say to me, "If you had just obeyed, we would not be in this situation right now." Or (I always loved this one): "Your language forces me to wash your mouth out with soap." There was always a consequence. I never got into trouble when I obeyed; but when I did not obey, consequences happened in my life.

God did not ask Jonah to do anything he was not familiar with. Jonah was a prophet. What did prophets do? They preached. They told people they needed to repent: "You are a dirty rotten ugly sinner. You are a sinner in the hands of an angry God. You have to repent of your ways." God was telling Jonah to do what Jonah did.

I am a pastor. General Motors will never be calling me to ask me to help with the engineering problems in their cars. God has gifted me in ways that He has not gifted you. He has gifted you in ways that He has not gifted me. He commanded Jonah to do something he was familiar with. He told Jonah to go to the Ninevites, show them grace, and preach to them. He was called to preach because he was a prophet.

There are a lot of times in our own lives when the Spirit of God moves in our hearts to minister to someone or to help someone and, like Jonah, we do not. There are times in our lives when we read the Bible and see a commandment like this one:

Jesus replied: "'Love the Lord your God with all your heart and with all your soul and with all your mind.' This is the first and greatest commandment. And the second is like it: 'Love your neighbor as yourself.'" (Matthew 22:37–39)

We read the very words of Jesus and somehow think it doesn't apply to us. Yet, who is my neighbor? My neighbor is the guy who just cut me off in traffic. My neighbor is the person in the McDonald's drive-through who won't look at me or say hello. My neighbor is my boss. My neighbor is the person who works next to me. My neighbors are those people who God has brought into my life who I interact with all of the time. When I have an opportunity to obey God and share my faith with them, do I do it? Am I really concerned about them? Do I love them as I love the Lord my God: with all my heart, with all my soul, with all my mind and with all my strength?

Jonah Obeys

Now Nineveh was a very important city—a visit required three days. (Jonah 3:3)

God did not tell Jonah he could go in there, preach, and then leave. He needed to stay for forty days. There was a lot of work that needed to be done. Jonah needed to go all over the city and share with them the news.

What did Jonah do? He preached God's message. On the first day, Jonah preached: "In forty days, Nineveh will be overturned!" This word *overturned* is the same verb used for the destruction of Sodom and Gomorrah. Jonah's message was not unclear. He did not say, "God loves you and has a wonderful plan for your life." He did not say, "Your best life now forever," or "Why can't we all just get along?" No, he said, "You have forty days. Forty days from now, Nineveh will be overturned." It was very clear. They needed to repent.

We read in the New International Version (1984) that God told Jonah to use eight words: "Forty more days and Nineveh will be overturned." More than likely, Jonah said other words than that. He preached and evangelized. He was doing what we would call sharing the gospel. The word *gospel* is not a religious word. It is actually a Greek word, *evangelion*, and it is often used in times of war.

In Sparta, the Spartans would go to war with a group of people. Most of the time, they would win. When they did, they would send back one person to Sparta who would run through the city and yell: "NIKE!" You know what that means? Victory!

What was Jonah doing when he came into the city? He was sharing the good news. You know what the good news is? The good news is the gospel. Jonah went into the city and yelled, "Forty more days—you had better repent! If not, God is going to overthrow this city." The city and the people were so cruel. Still, Jonah shared the good news in Nineveh.

The Ninevites Believed

In verse 5, it says, "The Ninevites believed God." That seems strange—Ninevites believing in God. That is like oil and water. Yet they believed and declared a fast, and all of them, from the greatest to the least, put on sackcloth.

When the news reached the king of Nineveh, he rose from his throne, took off his royal robes, covered himself with sackcloth and sat down in the dust. Then he issued a proclamation in Nineveh: "By the decree of the king and his nobles: Do not let any man or beast, herd or flock, taste anything; do not let them eat or drink. But let man and beast be covered with sackcloth. Let everyone call urgently on God. Let them give up their evil ways and their violence. Who knows? God may yet relent and with compassion turn from his fierce anger so that we will not perish." (3:6–9)

Nineveh drastically and dramatically repented. They believed God. It is similar to Saul coming to faith in Jesus Christ. It is like that family member who you just keep sharing Christ with while wondering, *Will God ever really save that person?* God can do it. Jonah was faithful bringing the gospel, and revival took place. It is not our role or our responsibility to decide when revival happens. It is the Holy Spirit who does that. It is the Spirit of God who opens eyes. It is the Spirit of God who opens ears. It is the Spirit of God who opens hearts so that people can understand the gospel of Jesus Christ. We never know what will happen when we share the gospel.

> It is not our role or our responsibility to decide when revival happens. It is the Holy Spirit who does that.

Jonah shared the gospel with a group of people that most had written off, including Jonah. To his own people, the Israelites, God had sent prophet after prophet, and they kept saying, "No." In this story, God sent a prophet to the Ninevites, a group of people who were not God's people, and they believed God. They repented and turned away from their wickedness. They turned away from the life that they had been living. They were cut to their hearts. They declared a fast, declaring to God their humility.

What is really interesting is what the king did. The king of Nineveh had to have been a fascinating individual, because the Ninevites (also known as the Assyrians) were some of the cruelest people during that time. The way they would go in and demolish entire groups of people was heartless, and yet it was always commissioned by the king of Nineveh.

But in this case, after hearing Jonah preach, it says he *rose* from his throne. That is an important term. Maybe the king rose out of reverence for God; maybe it was sorrow over sin. Not only did the king rise, it says that he took off his royal robes—not one robe but two robes. It was a sign of laying aside his throne and laying aside his robes for God.

Not only did he take off his robes, but also he covered himself with sackcloth. Sackcloth is not one of the real pretty outfits that you would put on during that time. It was made from goat's hair. It was not soft at all, but prickly and uncomfortable. During times of mourning, people in ancient times would sometimes tear their clothes and put on sackcloth out of reverence.

However, the king did not stop there. Next, he sat down in ashes. The king went away from his throne, took off his robes, put on sackcloth, and sat down in dust. When was the last time a king sat down in dust? One of the most powerful men of that time bowed his heart and his knees to God. This could only be the work of God in this man's life. *Humility* and *surrender* were probably not vocabulary words he learned growing up. The king was probably not one of those guys who often thought, *Man, I really need to be a little more humble in my affections toward my people.* I think he was the kind of guy who would shoot first and ask questions later.

He was similar to Peter in the New Testament. Peter usually jumped into situations head first (actually feet first, literally, into the water to walk to Jesus). He argued with God and said, "I will not deny you, Jesus."

"You are going to deny me."

"No, I'm not."

We see the kind of person that Peter and the king of Nineveh were, and we have to wonder to what extent did they understand surrender? To what extent did they understand humility? Yet, here was the king of Nineveh throwing everything aside, his entire kingdom, his entire throne, his robes, and he was sitting down in a pile of dirt.

The Proclamation of the King

God changed a Gentile's heart. Then the king issued a proclamation. Now, this is an interesting proclamation:

> *Then he issued a proclamation to Nineveh: "By the decree of the king and his nobles: Do not let any man or beast, herd or flock, taste anything; do*

not let them eat or drink. But let man and beast be covered with sackcloth. Let everyone call urgently on their God." (3:7–8)

I have often thought, *Why are the cows fasting? Why the herds? Why the animals? Why make them stop eating and declare fasts for them as well as put sackcloth on them?*

It is because the king was so serious about this revival that he was not going to let any stone be unturned. He did not care if you were an animal lover or not. He did not care if it was hot or cold. He wanted them to cover all of the animals. Cover them up. Cover them up so they wouldn't be judged by a holy God. The king was going to do everything that he could so that God would relent from His judgment against the Ninevites. It was not because the animals understood. They did not understand, but the king understood, and the king was concerned about His own life and about the lives of the people that he had been giving direction to.

He humbled himself and he made a statement:

"Let everyone call urgently on God. Let them give up their evil ways and their violence." (3:8)

What does "urgently" mean? It means with force: strength with might. The king was telling his people to pray *urgently*, with force. Cry out to God and get rid of your evil ways, so that God may relent from His anger and turn His anger away from them. The king knew to whom they needed to call.

Usually, the king answered all of the questions. The people would ask him for permission, "King, can I do this? King, do you think I should go kill these people?" Now the king was saying, "Do not call out to me. Call out to God. Do it with fervency. I want you to do it with might; I want you to do it with strength and stop sinning." This was the *king* talking. What a change! What caused that radical transformation? The work of God involved in a man's life.

The king goes on in verse 9 to say, "Who knows? God may yet relent and with compassion turn from his fierce anger so that we will not perish." Think about that. He did not want to die. He did not want his life to end like that. He did not want their lives to end like that.

God Loves to Save People

What did God do next?

When God saw that what they did and how they turned from their evil ways, he had compassion and he did not bring upon them the destruction that he had threatened them. (3:10)

God relented. God turned back. Jonah obeyed, Nineveh repented, and God relented. God did what God loves to do: He saved people. God loves to save people! God did not look forward to destroying Nineveh. God did not do that. He had compassion on them.

How would some of us have responded? *Zap!* "You're gone. You have been so cruel. You are so mean. You are so arrogant. You are so rude. You killed innocent people. You are gone!" What did God do? He had compassion on them and did not bring upon the destruction that He threatened on them.

What Does Jonah Have to Do with Jesus?

This is an incredible story of a man named Jonah, who was so much like you and me. He went into a place that did not really want to hear the gospel. They did not want to hear the good news. Still, he preached to them and they repented and their lives changed forever. My desire is that our hearts and lives are so impacted by Jesus Christ that we are compelled to go into our worlds and share the good news of Jesus Christ and that we would have the opportunity to see lives transformed by the power of the Spirit of God in a person.

My world is different than your world. God has called me into my specific missional living to reach out to a people who do not know Him. We should desire to be like a Jonah, except with a pure heart, and say, "I have a passion for your soul, because in forty days, or four months, or forty years your life could be overturned."

Jonah has been dead for a long time. As a matter of fact, his bones are probably dust right now. What does the story of Jonah have to do with Jesus? It has *everything* to do with Jesus:

126

Then some of the Pharisees and teachers of the law said to him, "Teacher, we want to see a miraculous sign from you." He answered, "A wicked and adulterous generation asks for a miraculous sign! But none will be given it except the sign of the prophet Jonah. For as Jonah was three days and three nights in the belly of a huge fish, so the Son of Man will be three days and three nights in the heart of the earth. The men of Nineveh will stand up at the judgment with this generation and condemn it; for they repented at the preaching of Jonah, and now one greater than Jonah is here." (Matthew 12:38–41)

The One that is greater than Jonah is Jesus. Christ was saying the story of Jonah was about Him. Three days, three nights—guess who that is about? That is about Jesus. This story about Jonah points to who Jesus is. Jonah was resurrected from the belly of that fish. Jesus Christ was resurrected from the dead. He is risen—He is risen indeed!

God Continues to Give Us Chances

The book of Jonah says that God is gracious, and because He is, He gives each one of us the opportunity to serve Him, even after we have blown it. Rejoice that God gives you that second, third, fourth, or even hundredth chance.

And do you know what God keeps doing? He keeps picking us up. He keeps forgiving us. He keeps pointing us to the cross and telling us to move forward. He gives us brothers and sisters and Christ to also pick us up and dust us off.

We need to focus our attention on Christ. If you have fallen, you can get back up. God *has* forgiven. God *is* forgiving. And He gives us the opportunity to repent of our sins. He helps us understand the wickedness of our ways and how great the offense of our sin is to His character and to His person. God is forgiving, and He shows it to a group of people that we would not forgive. We would kill them! We would destroy them all, like Sodom and Gomorrah. That is what I would have wanted to

> God keeps picking us up. He keeps forgiving us. He keeps pointing us to the cross and telling us to move forward.

see. Sometimes we will not say that out loud, but we think it in our hearts. *Did they really deserve God's forgiveness? Do I really deserve God's forgiveness?* No, but God is compassionate. When we realize the error of our ways He relents from the judgment we so richly deserve and provides us salvation we so desperately need with His Son, Jesus Christ. That is what God does.

The book of Jonah is not just another kid's story. The book of Jonah is a description of you and me. We do not *deserve* mercy, but we *receive* it. If you are not a follower of Jesus Christ, if your faith and your hope are found in anyone else other than Jesus Christ, then you are like those Ninevites before they believed God. You have no hope, you have no peace, unless your hope and your peace are found in the Savior, Jesus Christ. I would encourage you, I would beg you, and I would beseech you that you pray to the Savior, Jesus Christ, to save you, just as He saved the Ninevites.

Closing Prayer

Father, we are thankful for the fact that You used this prophet, Jonah, to go into a city and to preach a message that was foreign to them. Father, we are thankful they understood the Word, that they received the Word, and that a group of people like us put their faith and their hope in God. We pray that we would be passionate, that we would be deliberate in our worlds, that we would share Christ with people at the restaurant, in our homes, in our neighborhood, and at our schools. Father, we pray that we would see people come to faith in Christ and be grounded in Him. Thank you, God, that You relented and that You changed a group of people that we would say are worthless, without hope. But You did it in the book of Jonah, and You have done that with us. Help us, God, to live for You in everything we say and in everything we do. We pray this in the name of our Savior and our Lord, Jesus Christ. Amen.

April 18, 2010
Cornerstone Baptist Church

Chapter 11

JONAH THROWS A PITY PARTY

Jonah 4

Well, are you as excited as I am? Jonah chapter 4! It's like the anticipated Christmas. You can't wait for Christmas Eve to get over with so you can wake up early on Christmas day. Just like you've been looking forward to Jonah 4! For many of you, it's like the vacation you look forward to and anticipate. You're so excited. It's kind of like Jonah 4. For some of you anticipating your first AARP card (isn't that great?), it's kind of like Jonah 4. Or those of you who are getting your first Social "Insecurity" check and looking forward to that! Well, it's finally here! Jonah 4 is here! And, as Paul Harvey would say, "Now, I'm going to tell you the rest of the story."

But, before I do, I want to do a quick run-through of chapters one through three. So, this is a "Cliff's Notes" version of Jonah chapters 1, 2, and 3. Buckle up and hang on.

Review

Jonah was a prophet. He prophesied about three thousand years ago. God told him to go do some things, and we will see in a moment that he did not like that. A lot of people think that the themes of Jonah have to do with the fish and the worm and all of these other interesting things that we've seen on Veggie Tales or flannel graph. Really, Jonah is the theme of God's sovereignty. God is in control. And you see it all throughout the book. It's also a theme that God is going after His people *relentlessly*. He never gives up! He never stops! He is always going after His people.

In Jonah 1, God called Jonah to preach. That's what preachers do. They're to preach! But, He told him that He wanted him to go to a place called Nineveh. Nineveh was the capital of Assyria. We'll look at them a little bit later. But I would explain it simply as this: they were some bad people. They were rough. They were not part of God's chosen people. And, so Jonah decided, "I've got a better idea. I'm going to go two thousand miles away in another direction." He jumped into a boat and took off. He thought everything was good.

God sent a storm. The sailors realized after a while the storm was because of Jonah, so they threw him overboard. He was running from God, and what did God do? He provided a fish. In fact, at the end of Jonah 1, we found Jonah being swallowed by a huge fish sent by God.

In chapter 2, Jonah was in the belly of the fish. This wasn't your typical time-share resort: "Where am I going to go on vacation? I think I'll take a little trip in a marine animal that has lungs and gills and everything it just ate for lunch." This wasn't that type of trip. Jonah was in the middle of this fish, and he realized it was only God who could save him. He repented. He cried out to God and, at the end of chapter 2, we saw God making the fish vomit Jonah onto dry ground. That's a lovely picture!

In chapter 3, Jonah said, "Okay, I think I'm going to do it. I'm going to obey God." God gave him the message: "I want you to go up and down the streets, and I want you to tell the people of Nineveh that in forty days they're going to be overturned." Forty more days and Nineveh would be demolished. That was his message to them.

Now, we know he said other things as well, but it was basically, "You need to repent, you need to turn from your sin, and you need to accept God's love and forgiveness." They did! They repented! And when I say "they" repented, I mean *everybody* repented, from the king all the way down. They put on sackcloth, they fasted, and they hoped God would not destroy them. And that is where we left them at the end of Jonah 3.

Jonah Gets Angry

As chapter 4 begins, we now see a dialogue taking place between God and Jonah. And this chapter is divided into two sections. Let's start by reading the first, Jonah 4:1–3.

But Jonah was greatly displeased and became angry. He prayed to the Lord, "Oh, LORD, is this not what I said when I was still at home? That is why I was so quick to flee to Tarshish. I knew that you are a gracious and compassionate God, slow to anger and abounding in love; a God who relents from sending calamity. Now, O Lord, take away my life, for it is better for me to die than to live."

What? Jonah said he'd rather die than live? His language was very, very strong. Jonah was just flat out angry with God. It was not what he signed up for. His goal, his objective, was to go out and preach. And that's what preachers do. They preach. They tell the good news, and that's what Jonah did. But now we see in verse 1 that he was very displeased, very angry, and very frustrated. It's like this prophet was taking his fists, sticking them up in the sky, and saying, "Listen! This is not what I signed up for! I don't like what's taking place here! I don't like the fact that You saved all these people and that You're allowing them to repent! This is not what I wanted to do!"

"I Knew You Were Gracious"

Jonah made four statements here. He was like a lawyer. He was getting ready. He was building up his case. Jonah was calculating the things that He and God had talked about before. He said, "I said to You that I knew you were a gracious and compassionate God."

He was lecturing God. And, here, you see the heart of this guy named Jonah. Again, what are preachers supposed to do? They're to preach. Jonah was going to a place that he was not familiar with. Obviously, he had never been there before. He was going to a people that were not God's people. They were cruel and wicked. They killed people and they were racists.

Jonah was thinking, *They're not God's people, and if they're not God's people, I don't want to tell them the good news!* He was saying to God, "Look, I said to You earlier I don't like this! I don't want to have any part of this, God."

Jonah would rather hope for destruction than for deliverance. And God even told him what to preach! God didn't say to Jonah, "Go lock yourself in a room for about thirty hours and come up with a fantastic, evangelistic,

Billy Graham kind of message. Make sure you have all the props and visuals that you can, and just lay it out there."

No! "This is the message I want you to tell them: 'Forty more days and Nineveh will be overturned.'" That's not a message that you can mess up. Forty more days and they are done!

"I Was Quick to Flee"

So he was throwing his fists up in the air, and then he made another statement: "I was quick to flee." He was attacking God, lecturing Him: "I fled. I took off. This is not me."

A lot of times we think that by running from God, we can get away from Him. But He's still there. He's still chasing. I used to love playing hide-

> We think that by running from God, we can get away from Him. But He's still there. He's still chasing.

and-seek with my kids. We could be in the middle of the living room and they would say, "Let's play hide-and-seek." I'd say okay, and then they would take a blanket, put it over their heads, and lie in the middle of the floor. I hadn't moved, but they would think I didn't know where they were! I'd play along and say, "I don't know where you are!" They would start giggling, and the blanket would be shaking. They would think because they couldn't see me that I couldn't see them!

What was happening with Jonah was he was saying, "I'm taking off! I'm getting out of here! I want nothing to do with this!" As though if he ran from God, everything was going to be okay. He said, "I fled. I knew."

"You Are a God Who Relents from Sending Calamity"

He continued by saying, "I knew that you were a gracious and compassionate God and abounding in love; a God who relents from sending calamity." Jonah knew the truth! This verse is actually a quote from Exodus 34. So Jonah knew the Word. He obviously had taught the Word and lived it out. He said, "I know that's the kind of God that You are. I know that You're gracious, I know that You're compassionate."

Now, think about this. This was a prophet who was running from God, who obeyed God reluctantly, and then quoted to God how great He was:

"God, You are full of compassion, You are merciful, You are gracious, You are holy, You are righteous. You are all these things, but I want nothing to do with what You are telling me to do."

That's a little bit of a contrast from a prophet who you think would know better. See, Jonah knew that God was gracious to the guilty. Aren't you thankful for that? He is gracious to the guilty. Jonah knew that God was compassionate toward weak humanity, and we are described in Scripture in many different ways as sheep. We are described as grass that fades away. That's the way we're described! We're described as dirt! And yet God is compassionate toward weak humanity. God is slow to anger. He is abounding in love. He relents from sending calamity. And Jonah knew all of this!

Jonah could dot the *i*'s and cross the *t*'s. Jonah could give a theological lesson to anybody, yet inside of his heart, he was all about himself. He was fully self-absorbed, wanting to do life his own way. And God got in the way. Jonah refused to see the Assyrians the way God did. We will see, at the end of the chapter, that they did not know their right from their left. Now it doesn't mean that they didn't literally know: "Is this my right hand or my left hand? Man, I can't figure that out." No! It's not that they didn't know directionally, it's that they didn't know spiritually! They were dead! They were hopeless. They were sinners. When I come across somebody who doesn't know Christ, how do I see them? Do I see them through the lens of my arrogance, my own pride? Do I look at them and say, "Talk to the hand, don't get near me"? Or do I see people through the lens of Scripture? Do I look at people through the lens of God and what He wants me to see in them? And we know this! I live in the Detroit Metro area. It's not the nicest area in the world to live in. It's a little rough. People are a little mean. People are a little short. People cut you off every day. People like to do those things. It's part of who they are. How do I see them? Do I see them as people needing to understand their right hand from their left? Do I see these people as needing to understand the graciousness and the holiness of God? Or do I see them as a nuisance and say to them, "Get out of my life"?

"I Want to Die!"

Jonah did not want to go to Nineveh. He didn't want to preach, but he did, and God saved all these people. And then Jonah made this last statement. He

133

said, "I want to die." He would rather die than see the Ninevites come to faith in God. He would rather end his life. That's how serious it was. He would rather end his life than see an entire city come to faith in God. When we read Jonah's words, "I want to die," this isn't an easy term we glance over. It was his anger. It was his frustration. You see it throughout the whole book, and now he was saying to God, "I would rather *die* than see these people saved! I would rather end my life *right now* than to see Your grace work in their lives!" You talk about being *so* self-centered. His hatred is so deep. His hatred is so dark. His life is about himself and no one else. And God had gotten in his way. Basically, Jonah was saying, "God, I want You to do it *my* way."

My mom used to say, "It's *my* way or the highway!" The highway is a *long* way away! Even more reason it's *my* way! Oh. Okay. You know, Jonah had his own opinion of how God should act, and it angered him—it *truly* angered him—when God didn't act that way. How does that translate to my life and your life? Many of us think the same way that Jonah did, yet we don't even realize it. What might it look like for us? Here's an example of this thought process and how it might affect us today:

So, I've always been a list maker. Every big event, every big decision in my life, I get out my notebook and write out my list of requirements. All is right with the world when I can make my list and check things off. I really like my well-ordered life. For example, there was choosing a college. Not too big, check. Not too small, check. Not too far away, check. But certainly not too close, check! High academic ratings, check. Great facilities, check. Guy-to-girl ratio in my favor, check!

And choosing a job: Enjoyable work, check. Good pay, check. Good hours, check. Short commute, check. Enough vacation time, check. Room for advancement, check.

Then there was the husband list: A Christian, check. Smart, check. Good sense of humor, check. Responsible, check. Tall, dark, and handsome, check, check, check! Patient and kind, check. Easy going, check. Athletic, check. Musical and romantic . . . well, we can't have everything, I suppose.

The house list: Enough bedrooms, check. Enough bathrooms, check.

Quiet neighborhood, check. Enough square feet, check. Garage, check. Basement, check. Big yard, check. Updated, check. Right zip code, check. Right price, check.

The kids list: A boy, check. A girl, check. A nice school, check. Some nice friends, check. The best teachers, check. On the honor roll, check. College bound, check. Involved in sports, check. Involved in music, check. Involved in everything under the sun, check.

Picking a church: Right denomination, check. Not too big, check. Not too small, check. Not too long a drive, check. Something for the kids, check. Enough for the adults, check. Music: Not too old fashioned but not too crazy either, check, check. Preaching not too long . . . well, still getting over that one.

So, my life is pretty cut and dried. Pretty much the way I want it. Well, until I get to my God list. Now, I've never actually written it out on paper, but we certainly all have a list of requirements for God, right? He's supposed to be always loving, patient and kind, all powerful, seeing everything, knowing everything, fixing everything, keeping me joyful, happy, content, solving all my problems like helping me find my keys and making sure I get all the green lights when I'm in a hurry. He's supposed to keep me safe and healthy and protect my kids, protect my nice, little life.

But, here's where it gets sticky: I don't include on my list things like losing a job or being rejected. I don't include things like wars, terrorists, hunger, suffering. I don't include cancer or the death of a loved one. The abuse of a child. Those things just don't fit my picture of God. They certainly don't make my list. Somehow, it's not that simple. Somehow, God is not that cut and dried. Somehow, I don't think He's consulting my list.

Strike a chord? God did not fit in Jonah's box. God did not conform to Jonah's desires. God isn't a cosmic dispensing machine where you put a little money in, push the button, get what you want, and get a little change. A lot of times, we treat God like that. And Jonah was right at the pinnacle of treating God like that. He was actually looking up to God and saying, "We're going to do it my way and no other way."

135

God's Response

The second section of Jonah 4, verses 4 through 11, talks about God's response to Jonah's rebellion. God went after him. He went after him swiftly. He went after him aggressively. Verse 4 says, "But the Lord replied, 'Have you any right to be angry?'"

Jonah went out and sat down at a place east of the city. There, he made himself a shelter, sat in its shade, and waited to see what would happen to the city. Then God provided a vine and made it grow up over Jonah to give shade for his head and to ease his discomfort. Jonah was very happy about the vine. But, at dawn the next day, God sent a worm that chewed the vine so that it withered. When the sun rose, God sent a scorching east wind so that the sun blazed on Jonah's head so that he grew faint. He wanted to die and said, "It would be better for me to die than to live."

But God said to Jonah, "Do you have a right to be angry about the vine?"

> You see the response of God. He went after Jonah and convicted him with a question.

"I do," he said. "I am angry enough to die."

But the Lord said, "You have been concerned about this vine, but you did not tend it or make it grow. It sprang up overnight and died overnight." Then in verse 11 God tells Jonah, "But Nineveh has more than a hundred and twenty thousand people who cannot tell their right hand from their left, and many cattle as well. Should I not be concerned about that great city?" You see the response of God. He went after Jonah and convicted him with a question: "Do you have any right to be angry? Why are you upset that I've just shown my grace to an *entire* city?"

If our entire community came to faith in Christ, what would we do? We would throw a party! WE WOULD REJOICE! We would be thrilled and come along side of what God had done. Yet Jonah was so angry that he basically ignored God. God simply asked him a question and showed His graciousness to him. Look at verse 5 again: "And then Jonah went out and sat down at a place east of the city." How did he respond when God asked him a question? Jonah literally ignored Him! This was like having a conversation with a good friend who asks, "How's your day, Patrick?" and I just look at him, turn around, and walk away.

My Run-In with Mr. Gonzalez

When I was in fifth grade, I had a teacher by the name of Mr. Gonzalez. Mr. Gonzalez was a good fifth grade teacher, and every day during recess, we would play kickball. Now, just in case you're not too familiar with what kickball is, picture a baseball diamond with a pitcher's mound and home plate. What the pitcher would do is roll the ball, and the person at home plate would kick it to, hopefully, another county. So it was pretty simple. And then you would run the bases and try to get as many runs as you could. The team that had the most runs would win the game.

But Mr. Gonzalez had a couple of rules: First, he was the all-time pitcher. But he wasn't really a pitcher. He was like a bowler with an eight-ounce ball. So I would always go up to him and say, "Mr. Gonzalez, can I be the pitcher today?" He would say, "No. I'm the pitcher." He also had another rule: you never threw the ball to him or rolled the ball to him. You *handed* it to him. The guy ruled the class pretty well.

So one day, I decided to go up to him and ask again, "Can I be the pitcher?" He said, "No, you cannot be the pitcher." Every single day that I would ask him, I would get the same answer: "I am the pitcher." On this particular day, I got the ball and came over and saw that Mr. Gonzales was standing on home plate. And there was a brief temptation to take the ball and roll it. He looked at me, and I looked at him, and he said, "Hand me the ball." I looked at the ball, and the wise thing—the thing I should have done—would have been to honor him and hand it to him. I looked at home and thought, *This would be fun!* I stepped up a little bit closer, and he said, "Hand me the ball." And I took the ball, and I just rolled it.

Have you ever had an out-of-body experience where time stood still? He said, "DON'T KICK IT!" And everyone froze! I was in this out-of-body experience looking at all my friends thinking, *Wow!* Mr. Gonzalez grabbed me (you could do that back then). He corrected me (you could do *that* back then). And then he took his hand, brought it back as far as he could, and *WHAM!* He hit me right in the buttocks! I felt like I was lifted off the ground! (You could even do *that* back then too!) He said, "Let me tell you what, young man. When I tell you to give me that ball, you give it to me! I have rules for this class and you will follow them!"

He wasn't happy. My friends were snickering, and I was thinking, *Ooh, that kind of hurt. That wasn't too good.* Mr. Gonzales wasn't done. He said, "You go to Mr. Vine's office *right now!* You tell him *exactly* what took place, and *don't miss anything*, because I will follow up with him!"

So, I walked into the principal's office and said to the secretary, "I need to see Mr. Vine. Mr. Gonzalez sent me here." I'd been there a few times because the principal and I, well, we were like "good friends." Like Starsky and Hutch. I told him what happened. He corrected me and said, "Come here." He made me lean over in front of his table, and he took out a wooden paddle. And I'll tell you what. HE LIT ME UP! I was not a believer at that time, and I was praying for the Lord to return just at that moment! "Please, God, get me *outta* here!"

I went home. I walked into the house. My mom said, "Sit down. Sit down at the kitchen table." I knew the kitchen table was always the place where we did business together. And she said, "What happened at school? Don't you forget one single detail, because I've already talked to the principal!" I said, "Oh, man. All I did was throw a stupid little bouncy ball." She said, "You know what? That was not right. That was rude. That was mean. And now I'm going to spank you." *WHAM!* (But, you know, with my mom's spankings, it was nothing! I'm just glad my dad wasn't home, or that would have been a terrible, terrible day!)

Part of the problem was that Mr. Gonzales gave me a specific order, and I just flat out ignored him. I can laugh about it now. I'm sure all my friends were laughing about the fact that I got spanked that day. But Jonah's arrogance was even greater than my arrogance. Jonah turned around and walked in the complete opposite direction! He ignored *God!* So Jonah went out and sat down at a place east of the city. He made himself a shelter, sat in its shade, and wanted to see what God would do and what would happen to the city.

You might ask, "Why is he waiting?" I think he was waiting because he was hoping and he was expecting for God to still destroy the city. Jonah had some box seats. He had the good seats. He had the $300 seats. And he was waiting for God to not relent but to destroy the city. And I wonder if God had decided to destroy the city if Jonah would have been clapping.

"You guys deserved it over there! I saw you. I saw the way that you were acting. I saw the way you were treating everybody! This is a good day! *This* is the day that the Lord has made! I'm rejoicing because all of you have been nuked!" I'm wondering, would he be thankful for that? Would he be hoping, "Now, God, You and I can get back together. Now we can do business again. What's my next job? What do You want me to do?" I think he was waiting to see if God was going to destroy the city.

God Uses Nature to Reach Jonah

And then God, by His graciousness, provided a vine.

> *Then the Lord provided a vine and made it grow over Jonah to give him shade for his head to ease his discomfort. (4:6)*

And Jonah was very happy about the vine. He wasn't just happy. He was *very* happy. The days of the creation were *very* good. God created man. God is *very* good. God provides many things, and we see God providing several things in the story of Jonah. In chapter 1, He provided the wind. Then He sent a large fish to swallow and protect Jonah. Now He was sending a vine. Remember, this was a location that is modern-day Iran. It was extremely hot! There wasn't a lot of shade. This was just showing God's sovereignty. In God's creation, He can make *anything* out of what He has created.

> In God's creation, He can make anything out of what He has created.

So, if you're in the middle of the desert and God decides that He wants to create a vine, He can do it, because He's in control. He's using the creation to tell Jonah, "Listen, there's a problem with your thinking! You're not thinking biblically here. You're happy about a *vine!* You're content about a *vine!* You're more concerned about the vine than you are a hundred and twenty thousand people!"

You see the contrast here? Happy about a vine, angry with God about Nineveh.

> *But at dawn the next day, God provided a worm which chewed the vine so that it withered. (4:7)*

People ask the question, "How big was the worm?" Just watch Veggie Tales. It tells you all your theological truths! And he's cute! I don't know how big the worm was. I don't really care. It's not really a topic I'm concerned about. But I do know this: The worm had one objective. It was to kill the plant. Who gave the orders? God! What did the worm do? Obeyed! We're talking about a *worm!* We're talking about a *vine!* And so God was still using his creation saying, "Do you see the contrast? Do you realize there's a problem here, Jonah? On one hand, you're just thrilled about a vine, and on the other, you're angry about the fact that I have changed the lives of a hundred and twenty thousand people."

Then God provided a hot wind. Not just a wind. A *hot* wind. The sun rose and God provided a *scorching* east wind.

When the sun rose, God provided a scorching east wind, and the sun blazed on Jonah's head so that he grew faint. He wanted to die, and said, "It would be better for me to die than to live." (4:8)

God was once again trying to get Jonah's attention through His own creation. And God continued to go after him. Jonah was so focused on himself and so absorbed in himself that he said, "I just want my life to end." But God never gave up on him. Then God asked him a question again in verse 9: "Do you have a right to be angry about the vine?" What did Jonah do? He answered, not ignoring God anymore: "I do. I am angry enough to die."

God Never Gives Up

God continues to go after His people! God continued to show His graciousness to Jonah. Now, a lot of us at this point would not have been surprised to hear God say, "I'm done with you! Bzzz—You're gone, you are outta here! Come on! Anybody else want to question me? Stand up in line, let's go! One, two, three, four, come on—we'll get rid of all of you!" That's how we would have reacted to Jonah. But God didn't do that. He was gracious, and He continued to show His compassion. With Jonah, there was so much righteous anger that he has missed it completely. Rather than see the vine as a blessing, he got angry that it was gone. Rather than enjoy it for a time, he focused on the loss. Rather than learn a lesson, he had to endure great hardship: God sent wind, God sent waves, God sent a fish, God sent a vine, God sent a worm, God sent a hot, scorching wind. God did all of this trying to get Job's attention, saying, "I want you to be the prophet that you are supposed to be. I want you to tell people about God's love and God's forgiveness."

In verses 10 and 11, again God laid it out completely to him:

"You have been concerned about this vine, though you did not tend it or make it grow. It sprang up overnight and died overnight. But Nineveh has more than a hundred and twenty thousand people who cannot tell their right hand from their left, and many cattle as well. Should I not be concerned about that great city?"

Let me ask you some questions:

- Did Jonah plant the plant? *No!*
- Did he water it? *No!*
- Did he fertilize it? *No!*
- Did he pull the weeds around it? *No!*
- Did he own it? *NO!*
- Did he make it grow? *No! God did it all!*

Yet Jonah was more concerned about the vine than he was the people that God told him to reach. Here sat a man of God on the outskirts of a city filled with rage, anger, and frustration because God did not act the way Jonah wanted Him to act. So the story of Jonah ends with a question: "Should I not be concerned about that great city?"

Some people say Jonah repented and got right with God. Some say he didn't repent and didn't get right with God. We don't really know. There are assumptions that could be made either way. But I do know this: Jonah was to tell God's story. And when you look at the life of Jesus Christ compared to the life of Jonah, there's such a contrast. Jonah ran away from the city. Christ ran into the city. Jonah ran away from the people. Christ ran to the people.

What Jonah didn't do, Christ did. Jesus went into the city, He went to the people, and He humbly gave Himself up to everything. He died for those who do not know their right hand from their left. And that is the example we look to. That is the person we model our lives after.

Closing Prayer

Father, we are so thankful that You are in control, that You are sovereign. We thank You, God, for the message You have allowed us to share with people who do not know their right hand from their left. Lord, I pray that we would be diligent in doing that. And that, Lord, we would even look to the life of Jonah and realize how easy it would be for us to get our priorities confused and for us to think that we are in control when You are in control, for us to put our faith in something or someone other than You. Lord, we won't want to do that. I pray you would guard our hearts so we don't become so self-absorbed that we focus on ourselves. Lord, our desire, as followers of Jesus, is to bring attention to You and only You. And, Lord, we pray this in the magnificent name of our Lord and Savior, Jesus Christ. Amen.

April 3, 2011
Cornerstone Baptist Church

Resources

Patrick's Blog: www.PatricksStory.com

Read the journey of Patrick's last year of life, beginning with finding out about ALS and every step along the way. If this book has inspired you in some way to take a step toward Christ, we would love to hear about it. Please tell us in a comment on the blog at PatricksStory.com.

The McGoldrick Family Fund

Donations will be invested 100 percent for the benefit of the McGoldrick family—most of it to be used to help Paige and Parker with their college education.

- By credit or debit card: www.wepay.com/donations/mcgoldrick
- By check: Write your check to "Friends of Patrick & Dena McGoldrick" and mail it to Fifth Third Bank, 40980 Hayes Road, Clinton Township, MI 48038

Online Videos

- Patrick's Final Sermon: vimeo.com/41122112
- Celebration of Life Service: vimeo.com/57436072

Church

If you live in the area, we encourage you to visit the church where Patrick served for twelve years. The congregation truly showed the love of Jesus to the McGoldricks in a thousand ways during his sickness.

Cornerstone Baptist Church
17017 E 12 mile Road
Roseville, MI 48066
www.cbcroseville.org

From Patrick's Former Students

Patrick and Dena impacted literally hundreds of students over the years in Indiana, Kentucky, Illinois, and Michigan. Many of those students are now parents and church leaders. A few of them are expressing, on behalf of the rest, their gratefulness for the McGoldricks' impact.

Stephanie Dilley—Detroit, MI—Student: 2000–2002

My time in the youth group under Patrick and Dena's ministry forever changed my life, and I am incredibly blessed and honored to have been a part of their ministry. They have never wavered from their call to serve the Lord and His people.

Pastor Joseph DiVietro—Wilson, KS—Student: 1990–1995

Patrick and Dena were so influential to me at one of the worst times of my life as a teen. During my parents' move and divorce, it was their ministry and hospitality that the Lord used to keep me on track! Numerous lives have been affected for eternity through the ministry I have today because of what the McGoldricks did back then.

Dave and Cara Farrell—Beavercreek, OH—Students: 1996–1998

It is hard to quantify in words what the ministry and lives of Patrick and Dena McGoldrick have meant to my wife and me. They have been shining examples of faith, perseverance, integrity, and love. From nurturing us through high school, our marriage, and as we started a family, they stood beside us through their support and example. Martin Luther King, Jr., once said, "The ultimate measure of a man is not where he stands in moments of comfort and convenience, but where he stands at times of challenge and controversy." Truly, as Patrick faced ALS and maintained his faith, his joy, and his love for the Lord, he demonstrated the measure of what a great man he was and a shining example of

Christ. Few people I have known have ever left a legacy that will last for so long with such a great impact as Patrick had.

Jonathan Farrell—Morton, IL—Student: 1993–1998

I'm thankful to Patrick & Dena for selflessly loving our King and serving Him in the local church! As the Ray Boltz song describes (which we performed on numerous missions trips!), mine is a life that has been forever changed.

Ryan Gasparotto—Harper Woods, MI—Student: 1999–2003

I am forever grateful for the impact Patrick has had on my life as a pastor, teacher, mentor, and friend.

John Hicks—Three Rivers, MI—Student: 2000–2005

I can't thank Patrick enough for the impact he had on my walk with Christ. The time and wisdom he invested in me still affects my life and ministry on a daily basis. I am confident that the work he did for Christ will continue to multiply and reach generation after generation for His glory. I'm grateful for his powerful example of faithfulness to our great God!

Katie Horton—Gaylord, MI—Student: 2000–2004

Patrick and Dena were like second parents to me. I always looked up to their marriage and always wanted to have the same one day. Being married now, I especially strive to have that and pray that Daniel and I will always take our vows in the same way that I saw in Patrick and Dena. I love you!

Michelle Klassen Jones—St. Louis, MO—Student: 1990–1996

Patrick and Dena were the biggest spiritual influencers of my life. They taught and lived Christ for all of us. I can never thank them enough— their passion for Christ and love for each other changed so many. God was so kind to allow me to be under their teaching.

Micah Manore—Joliet, IL—Student: 2002–2004

I disagreed with Patrick a lot when I was in high school. I've spent the last decade of my life, education, and ministry realizing he was pretty much right.

Thomas Nelson—Birmingham, AL—Student: 1998

Pastor Pat put all his energy into investing in us. It wasn't for show but a genuine concern for our spiritual well-being. It pays eternal dividends, for which I'll always be grateful.

Jeremy Pearson—Warren, MI—Student: 2001–2007

Patrick has shaped how I will live, love, and do ministry in the future. I have many times in the past and will continue to ask myself for the rest of my life, "What would Patrick say to me right now?" His love for those who he served and his huge smile and joy will never be forgotten.

Nicole Albright Peterson—Dickson City, PA—Student: 2002–2008

Whether it was encouraging me to jump into uncomfortable situations with both feet or challenging me to be the leader he saw I could become, Patrick led a life I knew I wanted. Now living life in the ministry as a youth pastor's wife, I try to give students a glimpse of Patrick McGoldrick.

Rebecca Phillips—Chattanooga, TN—Student: 1997

I was a teenage girl struggling with doubt and confusion about salvation and all things biblical. Pastor Pat spoke truth in an effective way and brought stability to my thought processes. While being the cutest dresser ever and coolest person I'd ever met, Dena took an interest in my walk with Christ and encouraged me to study the Word. I'll never forget the day Pastor Pat baptized me. It was different from the times he dove for my legs and dragged me under water at camp, but the same strength lifted me from the water, and I walked away knowing my "newness of life."

Allison Secrest Walters—Lexington, KY—Student: 1992–1998

Pastor Pat and Dena were (and will always remain) more influential and more beloved in my youth than any other individual or couple, other than my parents. I not only had the privilege to sit under their teaching for six years in the youth group but was privileged to live with them during my senior year of high school. Their grace, love, and generosity to me will never be forgotten, and my love and gratitude for them runs deeply. Their example of a Christ-exalting, gospel-centered marriage, and their godly, Bible-saturated parenting shapes the way I live today.

Noah Young—Detroit, MI—Student: 1992–1996

Pastor Pat and Dena poured themselves selflessly into my peers and me. We saw firsthand their love for Jesus, each other, and us. Whether going to summer camp, Teen Leadership Conference, Winter Retreat, or just coming to my public high school for lunch, Patrick cared about my friends and me. My life, and now my family, has been blessed beyond measure by the influence of Patrick and Dena. My love and prayers are with them daily.

From Patrick's Former Interns

Patrick was known as a discipler of men. In fact, every year he would search the country for one man to spend the year as a youth ministry intern. He wasn't looking for someone to do his grunt work—he was looking for a man who wanted to go deep in his faith and far in his ministry. These men, and the ministry they represent, have become a part of his lasting legacy.

Chip Dean—Harvest, AL—Intern: 2001–2002

Through Patrick and his ministry, God radically changed my life and ministry! During my internship, I learned unbelievably valuable and practical tools for student ministry. Patrick empowered, challenged, encouraged, corrected, trained, and equipped me. I will be forever thankful for his weekly Tuesday morning intern evaluation meetings with me. He entrusted the middle school ministry to me, which gave me the experience I needed to be on my own. Now, I get to tell people all the time that my youth ministry is basically a rip-off of Patrick's. All about the gospel of Jesus, just like he taught me!

Andrew Dodd—Hammanskraal, South Africa—Intern: 2004–2005

When I think about Patrick, three words quickly come to mind: leader, mentor, and friend. Wherever Patrick was, people looked to him for insight and answers. John Maxwell defines leadership as "influence—nothing more, nothing less." This truly is a fitting definition of Patrick. I cannot begin to count all of the things taught and caught during my time as an intern. He showed me that ministry is all about relationships. His heart and passion for reaching students with the life-changing truth of the gospel continues to be an example to me. Thank you, Patrick, for your friendship and for teaching me to run harder after Christ.

Chad Holmgren—Eastpointe, MI—Intern: 2005–2006

I have known Patrick for seven years. The first time I met with Patrick in his office, it was apparent that he had great interest in golf and an even greater interest in people. It wasn't long into our first conversation that I felt like Patrick was a friend whom I'd known much longer than a few minutes. Over the years, Patrick proved to be more than a friend. He was a shepherd. The example he set for young men as a husband, father, and pastor had an impact for the kingdom that will not be fully realized in this life. I will always be grateful for the investment Patrick made in my life.

Steve Garcia—Akron, OH—Intern: 2000–2001

Patrick was always a great teacher. He taught me much through his ministry, but even more so through his affliction.

Bobby Johnson—Louisville, KY—Intern: 2009–2010

I was sitting in youth group in 7th grade. I remember a couple different guys Cornerstone was considering as youth pastor, but when Patrick came and spoke and gave his testimony that first time, he had us all locked in. From then on, getting to know Patrick was a gift from God. From the all-nighters to Buford to Jamaica, Patrick was providing a way for his students to excel spiritually. The year I graduated high school, five of us from his youth group went to Bible college. I returned to be his intern in 2009, and the invaluable lessons of serving alongside him and seeing his consistent passion to run hard after Christ will stick with me for a lifetime but will be passed on to those God entrusts me with.

Johnny Norbeck—Roseville, MI—Intern: 2002–2003

"For none of us lives to himself, and none of us dies to himself. For if we live, we live to the Lord, and if we die, we die to the Lord. So then, whether we live or whether we die, we are the Lord's." (Romans 14:7–8 ESV)

Patrick was always a model of these verses to me. He exemplified what it means to pursue Christ and to be Christ to others. He was a prime influence in my life—as a Christian, husband, father, and friend. Patrick was a great friend, faithful brother, and a worthy mentor.

Caleb McClarren—Morton, IL—Intern: 2007–2008

"Enduring." This is the word that sums up Patrick's life and ministry. Few days pass that I don't try to mimic his example, draw from his wisdom, or happen to meet someone else who has been impacted—directly or indirectly—by his faithful dedication to Jesus. Many youth pastors set their hands to the plow; very few finish the task to which they were called; and fewer still successfully train others to walk the furrow behind them. Patrick did just that, over and over again. We all stand on the shoulders of those who have gone before. For me, and for many others, those shoulders belong to a man named Patrick. Patrick—by the grace of Jesus Christ—had an enduring impact, and I am forever thankful.

Kevin Root—Denver, CO—Intern: 2008–2009

The heart of Patrick's and Dena's ministry was a passion to see students grow to love Christ and surrender their lives to Him. Patrick took seriously Scripture's command to make disciples and, starting with his own children, oriented his life toward leaving behind a generation of students that would impact the world for Jesus. He had a special knack for keeping the bar high on his expectations for students while keeping the entry bar low and the journey toward maturity full of love and grace. The world is only beginning to see the effects of Patrick's ministry.

Kerry John Weishaupt—Oshkosh, WI—Intern: 2006–2007

There have been many people in my life who I have learned from, few people in my life that I have wanted to learn from, but one man that I will always regret not learning more from. Patrick played many roles in my life: from youth pastor to boss, from boss to friend, and finally friend to brother. Many people will say God used Patrick in their lives, and I would second that. But I would also like to take it further: Patrick has and will continue to impact my life until the day I die. His words will echo in my mind, his actions will continue on in my memories, but most importantly his Savior and Lord will forever reign in my life. To God be the glory!

Evan Whiteaker—Louisville, KY—Intern: 2011–2012

I count it a joy and a blessing to have been a part of Patrick and Dena's ministry while being a student and intern. Patrick taught me what it means to be a man of God, and that is one of the reasons I want to be a youth pastor. Even after being diagnosed with ALS, Patrick did not waver in his faith but trusted God even more. Seeing Patrick and Dena live out their faith in the hardest times has been an example to me.

18742612R00087

Made in the USA
Charleston, SC
18 April 2013